CW00853159

Introduction

Why do you want to be a nurse? This was the first question slung at me from out of the blue by a hard faced matron. I had expected questions concerning educational qualifications, personal details and background, but not for one moment had I imagined anyone asking me why I wanted to be a nurse. Of course, I had no answer and sat there wondering whether I should make something up about being called to a noble profession but decided it wouldn't wash, so I just sat open mouthed. Why did I want to be a nurse anyway? I didn't know, I just did, and had done from the age of 14.

After that the questions came thick and fast and I emerged with no clear details of the interview, but with the feeling of having battled through a dense jungle. Some days later there was a brief letter saying I had been accepted for training, and a list as long as my arm of text books, name tapes and other money consuming items. My heart sank, there was three shillings and sixpence in my bank account and about four and five pence in my handbag. A state of affairs to which I became accustomed in the following three years. One by one I obtained all the items on the list, the most spectacular of which was a massive canvas laundry bag with my full name emblazoned in scarlet letters right across the front and back. This laundry bag served me faithfully during my training and eventually ended up as a shroud for a pet puppy, buried two or three feet deep in Cypriot soil while EOKA bombs rattled the house, but that is another story

Experience is the only real teacher and looking back on the years spent in the nursing profession, happy years, yes, now looking as it were from a distance, I can say they were happy years. Sometimes hectic, sometimes heartbreaking, but they were happy. A look here, a word there, all these leave their mark and at the end emerges a nurse. In this book I am going to record people and events as they come to mind and try and build up a picture, however disjointed, of a nurse training in the late 50's early 60's.

Chapter 1

One of the first things I recall about my nursing career was 'junior nights' so many memorable things seemed to happen in a short space of three months. There was the time when I was left in charge of Miller ward while my senior went off to a meal break. Feeling quite important I strolled up the ward to check that everyone was peacefully asleep. It was a long ward, partitioned off with windows in the roof and the moon shone in silver patches through these. I neared the end of the ward and nothing was amiss, then suddenly I froze. There in front of me was the most hair raising sight imaginable. In a patch of moonlight, waist length silver hair glowing eerily was a figure, all of six feet in height, stark naked and coming slowly towards me. Mrs Davies had discarded her nightie and was sleepwalking. A logical enough explanation but at

2am, alone on your first spell of night duty, well, just imagine it. For weeks after, that patient would tell everyone, doctors and patients alike how she had frightened little nurse Jenkins.

Then there was the case of Mary Parsons, a lovable, fluffy and feminine patient. She was admitted to the ward with a slipped disc. The treatment at the time was by traction, a process whereby weights were attached to a pulley and fixed to Mary's heels in order to obtain the maximum rest for her back. The problem was that Mary was addicted to wearing very frilly fancy undies and insisted on having the traction disconnected twice a day in order to change them. I never found out if her back healed completely, but if it did, rest could not have been a factor.

Children make amusing patients. A young lad called Tim came to 'casualty' to have a painful boil lanced. We prepared to administer the anaesthetic but Tim burst into floods of angry tears, he was not going to have 'an ole black cup' over his face. All we could say by way of persuasion was of no avail. Tim's mother was called in and tried pleading and threats with no effect. Suddenly the Senior Consultant strolled in, alerted by the noise. He summed up the scene at a glance. "Hello young feller, how about a ride in a space ship." The little boy stopped crying and looked suspiciously at this elderly distinguished gentleman. "Where is it then?" he said, obvious disbelief in his voice. "Right here m'boy," and, delving into a cupboard he pulled out what looked like a glass cylinder, then another. "You put 'em over your head like this," he said and proceeded to place the object to rest on his massive shoulders. Tim, all fear forgotten did likewise, then the 'chief' signalled to the anaesthetist to attach one tube to his own mask and one to Tim's. "Got to have oxygen, you see," he explained. Within minutes Tim was peacefully asleep and the boil was lanced and dressed.

Adults who object to having anaesthetics are a different proposition however. Mr Jensen was admitted to male surgical ward with a large duodenal ulcer. He had had it for years and had learned to live with it. By careful dieting and a quiet way of life he had done much to reduce the discomfort it could cause. Lately it had been troubling him a great deal causing loss of sleep and constant pain. He came into hospital and after various tests the doctor advised a partial gastrectomy. To everyone's surprise, Mr Jensen flatly refused any surgical intervention. Being a practical and sensible man in all other respects everyone thought he would agree that this was the only lasting solution. "It's like this, nurse," he explained one evening as I was making his bed. "That thing never really bothered me before and I'm fair terrified of the gas." He remained adamant and we did what we could in the way of conservative treatment. A few nights later my junior came hurrying to tell me that he was showing all the signs of collapse and vomiting blood. Yes, the ulcer had perforated, and in spite of all we could do, we couldn't save him. Had we failed, we wondered, in stressing the serious need for an operation? We will never know. Of course, these days there are drugs to ensure things do not reach that stage.

Some patients, especially those who have been in hospital a long time become very shrewd in summing up a nurse. We overhear some rather revealing things sometimes, little things such as, "don't ask Nurse Morgan for a drink, she'll forget." This to a new patient, or, "See Nurse Jeffries, she wants to be a missionary in China. Won't make it though, no perseverance." Sometimes between a nurse and her patient there springs up a kind of unspoken bond, you get to anticipate their needs and are able to give them reassurance. This is not usual, but when it happens it is an experience that makes all the hard work and sheer drudgery worthwhile. Yes, there is a definite bond between nurse and patient, and if the nurse is moved to another ward she feels a little sense of loss. There was a dear old man who had been ill for many years on my ward and I was a very junior nurse. Sister was in a particularly venomous mood and chose me to be the victim of her wrath (or so I thought). I was attending to old Mr Venables and trying my best to look normal when underneath I was seething because Sister had told me I looked as if I had been dragged through a hedge backwards. As I was puffing up his pillows he caught my wrist and said, "never mind nurse you'll be a sister yourself one day." Just a simple sentence but it was just what I needed and, after all, I reflected, maybe my cap wasn't as neat as it might have been.

Time and again through my training I proved that the thing one dreads is never so bad when it happens. This was particularly so in what I called 'the haunted ward'. If there was one thing that all first year nurses dreaded, it was doing a spell of duty on Miller ward. The hospital had been badly blitzed during the war and the north wing had been reduced to a ruin. It was gradually being rebuilt but the signs of devastation could be clearly seen. Miller ward was at the end of a long dark corridor, and all around this part of the hospital there were grotesque ruins, holes and shadows. The night sister was a fiend for saving electricity and she would not allow this corridor to be lit. To go on and off duty and to meals the poor frightened nurse had to walk the length of this corridor, some fifty yards (these days things are measured in metres) holding her breath and afraid to look behind her. The stories that built up around that wing of the hospital were as numerous as they were fantastic. There were whispers of a grey lady in wartime auxiliary's uniform who pushed a trolley up the corridor in the dead of night. Some of my colleagues even went so far as to say they heard the trolley.

When I saw on the notice board that my name was down to go on night duty on Miller ward, you can imagine my feelings. The first night on duty I remember standing in the sluice, literally shaking and afraid to turn around. I had my back to the door and at the slightest rustle of sound I would jump. I distinctly remember praying that no one would call 'nurse' because I was too frightened to go into the ward, but this feeling passed with time. It seemed that every time the nurses gathered in the common room the conversation would turn, with morbid fascination to my ward. I can see now that the girls vied with each other in inventing stories to frighten me. One night I happened to mention that I could hear a tapping sound coming from the direction of the ante room adjoining the corridor. The story they told me to explain this phenomenon chills me even to this day. It seemed that a nurse was engaged to a young man who was terminally ill in the hospital. When the end came, they called the nurse to be with him. Hours later she did not return to her room in the nurses home, and eventually they found her body hanging in the ante room. The tapping noise was made by her feet as she swung to and fro. My friends assured me that the noise had been heard in Miller ward ever since. I was so scared that night that I flatly refused to go on duty unless a porter came and sat with me.

George, the porter was one of the kindest and most helpful men I met in the whole of my time at the hospital. He would go out of his way to do anything to make a very new nurse less homesick. He would talk for hours, and in the end I found myself forgetting all the ghastly stories and joining in his laughter. It was George who unearthed the cause of the tapping in the ante room. All the charts were kept there and there were some papers attached to a board with a clip on the wall. When the window was partly open the breeze would blow the board against the wall. Just a little sound, but when are on a ward in the dead of night with weird tales racing through your mind things assume immense proportions. It was George too, who nearly caused my most embarrassing moment. It was a few years later when I was a senior nurse and striving to maintain the dignity which befitted my position. There were gigantic wicker laundry baskets kept outside the Operating theatre, and George was unloading them into the lift. I was standing idly by, when George and another porter lifted me bodily into the laundry basket, shut the lid and pressed the lift button. Up came the lift and I was bundled into it protesting loudly. It descended with George sitting on the lid and the other porter standing by. Now this was a grand joke, and I didn't really mind, but when Matron and a hospital governor got in at the next floor it was a different matter. George just had time to whisper, "quiet, Matron," before she was in the lift. I hardly dared to breathe until she got out. Needless to say, I didn't lark about in laundry baskets any more.

One comes across many strange contradictions in human nature. There was the case of a young boxer who came to outpatients for an injection. He was a fine figure of a man, very tall with broad shoulders, a big red beard, sporting a yellow waistcoat and looking every inch a He Man. When he saw the needle, a tiny thing not two inches long, he swallowed hard and fainted. Maybe it was cruel to laugh, but I must confess I chuckled to myself. On the other hand, there was a frail and tiny woman, the mother of a large family, who had been ill with an incurable disease for a long time. The fortitude that woman displayed was amazing. She clung tenaciously to life with an almost visible effort. "Sheer guts is keeping Mrs Lindon alive." I heard the chief say on more than one occasion. There is an old superstition that says 'one in, one out', meaning that when an older person dies a new baby comes along. Mrs Lindon was waiting for the arrival of the latest grandchild and then she could leave in peace, and that is what happened.

My time as theatre escort was varied and interesting and I recall one incident in particular that amused me. The job of theatre escort was to take unconscious patients back to their respective wards after surgery. We had a casualty patient brought in, a teenage boy who had met with an accident. A dumper had fallen on him and he had serious injuries to his chest and stomach. He was deeply unconscious when George wheeled him into Casualty Theatre. An emergency splenectomy was performed and a blood transfusion set up. I was taking him to the ward on a trolley when he started to come round. He obviously couldn't remember what had happened, and all that registered in his mind was that he was being taken somewhere and his arm was strapped down. To my horror he started to struggle and kick and tried to wrench the transfusion from his arm, all the while emitting such a stream of foul language that even George began to look embarrassed. We had to enlist the help of a couple of medical students to get him into bed, where, suitably drugged, he slept it off. Weeks later, it was a shame faced Sid who told me that he thought he was being, "taken to the nick for being drunk."

The things people say when they are coming round from an anaesthetic would fill a book. I remember a teenager who developed a tremendous crush on the senior house surgeon. She used to tell me at great length how fabulous he was, and what he had said to her when he came to the ward. I was there when she went up for her operation, a simple appendicectomy. In the ante room after it was over, we were standing by the trolley when she opened her eyes wide, looked straight up at Alan, the Houseman and said in a voice full of hero worship. "I think you're wonderful." Then she went straight back to sleep. "So now you know," I grinned. For quite some time afterwards somebody or other would strike up a few bars of, "Mr Wonderful," whenever Alan entered the room.

Another time I escorted a schoolteacher out from theatre after his operation. As he was coming round he sat bolt upright on the trolley and began to make a speech in powerful ringing tones. "As I stand here before my maker," he began, and got no further for, as he saw me in a mask and gown he let out a yell of fright. He apologised profusely later on and was very embarrassed about it all. It still amuses me when I think about it. There was a blind old lady who came in with a fractured femur. She really was a dear and we were all very fond of her, she knew us all individually although she couldn't see us. Her visitors were sitting around her bed one afternoon when I came up with her tea. With so many people moving in the ward she didn't hear me. I smiled when I heard her say, "don't tell the nurse, but take these tablets 'ome, they baint doing me no good." The visitors looked as if they would like the ground to open up and swallow them, but I motioned them to pretend that I hadn't heard so that gran wouldn't feel awkward. Afterwards I explained to them what the tablets were and told them not to be partners in the old lady's crime. After that I kept a careful watch on her medication.

My time in the outpatients clinic was really hectic. It was a succession of people, people and more people. There were clinics from 9am until 4pm covering everything ranging from psychiatry to diabetes. The diabetic clinic was especially busy as the nurse had to arrange the patients's medical notes, weigh them, test the specimens of urine they brought, and if no specimen was forthcoming she had to show them where to go and provide them with a labelled bottle. All this in addition to answering patients queries and dealing with the doctors idiosyncrasies. One particular incident stands out in my mind amid all the jumble of these clinics. A gigantic young woman handed a specimen of urine to me to be tested for sugar and ketones. I duly tested it and found a large amount of sugar. This, I recorded on her chart and promptly dismissed it from my mind. Later an irate voice sounded from the consulting room. "Nurse, come here." I obeyed. "What's this?" said the doctor, tapping the woman's chart with his hand. "Sugar plus," I said brightly. "So I see," he said. "You realise, of course that Mrs Gibson's diabetes is quite stabilised now and she has had no sugar for ten months. Go and do it again." This I did, although there was a queue of patients waiting with their specimens and cards. Again I found sugar plus. Quite worried now - not so much about the state of Mrs Gibson but about Dr Pirie's sarcasm. I was just about to take the specimen to show him, when some instinct told me to look at the bottle containing the urine. Sure enough it had once contained children's cherry flavoured cough medicine, and the cork had not been washed, hence the sugar. Dr Pirie was satisfied, I was exonerated, and Mrs Gibson was delighted.

While we are on the subject of urine testing I must record something else that happened on 'junior nights'. There were three adjoining small wards with one large kitchen for the three. The night nurses for these wards would meet in the kitchen for a coffee and chat most nights. The talk got round to diagnosis by urine testing and we all agreed that because we were overtired and overworked, there would be a trace of albumin in our urine if tested. The next night we all brought a specimen just to satisfy our curiosity. The results were hardly what we expected. Grace, my colleague, had albumin in large quantities, which could be evidence of something quite serious, Joan had a neutral reaction, meaning that her urine was neither acid nor alkaline. We never could fathom out the significance of that, and I had a trace of sugar in mine. We were quite concerned for a time, but later tests we made all proved negative and we are all in the best of health to this day. Grace is a midwife, Joan is a ward sister, and I am a wife and mother cum practice nurse.

If there was one thing that I was to learn during my training, it was not to be surprised at the unexpected things. For example, there was a man admitted to the medical ward for investigations to find out why his kidneys were not functioning properly. He had high blood pressure that resisted all efforts to control it. All the necessary tests were made with no obvious result, as far as could be ascertained, his kidneys were normal. The Houseman decided to do an intravenous pyelogram, that is, to inject a radio opaque dye into his vein so that any abnormality would be shown up on an X ray film. This is where the unexpected happened. Mr Bainton had only one kidney and it was doing the work of two, and had been for 54 years. Hence the symptoms. When we told him this he was dumbfounded, no one had ever suspected it. All we heard from Mr Bainton for weeks after was, "well, fancy! Only one kidney." He would sit up in bed and repeat this profound remark to the ward in general and nobody in particular about twenty times a day.

Another time when the unexpected caught up with us was in the operating theatre. A woman had been brought in with severe pain in her lower abdomen, a rapid pulse and signs of shock. She was prepared for theatre as an emergency and the operation commenced, with the object of finding out the cause of her condition. Laparotomy revealed an appendix abscess which was duly removed and the patient recovered. All normal? Yes, but the unexpected thing was the fact that Mary had had her appendix removed ten years previously, according to her medical history. We could never get to the bottom of this particular mystery. Either the surgeon had removed something else, though there was no evidence to support this theory except a different laparotomy scar, or the appendix grew again, which is virtually unheard of.

Chapter 2

"Matron is doing a round." Those words stuck terror into the heart of many a junior nurse. There would be a frantic scuffling around to get all the beds and lockers in line, ash trays emptied and magazines tidied away. The Matron at my training hospital was a formidable person indeed. She would do a round of the Wards with Sister and chat to the patients, without apparently noticing the nurses, yet, when the ward round was finished she would mention to sister any little detail that was amiss with either the ward or our uniform. We often used to wonder if she had more than one pair of eyes, and would sometimes speculate as to where they were hidden.

Mr Barrat was gigantic, he was also arthritic. There were two nurses on duty the morning he decided to take a bath. Being stiff in his joints he had great difficulty getting in and out of the bath, and that morning he failed completely. Nurse

Morgan and I both pulled and pushed to the point of exhaustion, but we simply couldn't get him out. In the end we had to enlist Sister's help. With her vast experience of using a minimum force against a maximum load we managed to free Mr Barrat, but in the process, Sister's muslin cap fell in the water. Normally this would have been a minor mishap, but at that moment a shout was heard. "Matron is doing a round." Of course, a Ward Sister couldn't possibly do a round with Matron, minus her cap, and Matron could not excuse such gross inefficiency as to drop a cap in the bath. What was Sister to do? What she actually did was to send me rushing upstairs to the ward Matron had just left to borrow that Sister's cap. I arrived back just as Matron was within a few feet of the ward, and that saved the day.

Tradition dies hard in a hospital, and for generations the student nurses had worn their caps folded in a particular way, with one or two well placed tucks to make them smaller. The new Matron, after a conference with the board of governors, made it known that all caps should be of a regulation size, with no tucks or folds. This news was greeted with shocked horror and out and out rebellion by the main body of the student nurses. It was the general opinion that, after the storm had died down Matron would forget about the caps, so nobody took any notice. Matron didn't forget. After a few ward rounds when unsuspecting student nurses had their caps whipped from their heads and examined for pleats and folds, it began to dawn on them that she meant business. Eventually, after repeated notices on the boards, indoctrination by Sister and others in authority, and a few individuals being singled out for examples, about half the nurses altered their caps. This incident occurred towards the end of my training so I never found out how it all ended, but I must confess, if I were to return to my training hospital to see overlarge, cumbersome and stiffly starched caps, I would feel a mild disappointment.

One hears many stories about the operating theatre and it was with a great sense of awe that I began my first day there. I had expected stifling heat, complete heavy silence, except for the sharp demands of the surgeon, and the metallic slap as the instruments are pressed into his hand. Nothing could be further from the truth. As I stood there in the theatre on my first day, it was not unduly hot, the lights had not the glare that I had expected, and as for the heavy silence, there was more jovial chatter than could be heard even in the nurses common room. There was banter about last nights staff ball, and gossip as to the pending engagement of Sister Mason and Doctor Oswald. In fact, the atmosphere was nothing like I thought it would be. I had heard, too that the strain of working in the operating theatre would often cause young nurses to faint from heat and fatigue. In fact, the only person who fainted all the time I was working in theatre was a doctor of many years standing.

The nurse meets many different kinds of people, and here and there a personality is so strong that it stamps itself indelibly on her mind. One such person was Professor Robertson, he seemed to radiate electricity. He affected people in such a way that they either loved him or detested him. He had a knack of making a person feel about three inches high, and seemed to have the ability to see right into their thoughts. Professor Robertson was very brusque, even brutal in his dealings with patients, and yet, if he made a diagnosis, there was never any question of its accuracy. He was something of a showman, and invariably wore a single red rose in his buttonhole. Doctor Grant was another showman. Practically every nurse in the hospital had, at some time or another had romantic dreams about him. He bore an unusual likeness to Frank Sinatra, and he was well aware of this fact. He would stand by the blackboard, immaculately groomed, and pick up the chalk gingerly between his thumb and forefinger as if it were sacrilege to get a speck of chalk dust on his suit. When he picked up the duster he would bend forward from the waist, take it in the tips of his fingers as if not wishing to soil his hands, and wipe the board, standing as far away as the length of his arms would allow. He wore a different suit for every lecture. By direct contrast there was Doctor Meadows. He was never tidy or even reasonably well groomed. There never any suggestion of a crease in his trousers, and his hair was always a shade too long. On several occasions he was observed wearing odd cufflinks, and often wore odd socks. Yet he, in his way, had a kind of charm, and he was an excellent surgeon. Sarcasm was one of his bad points. He had an extremely cutting tongue. I was assisting at a minor operation one afternoon, an operation that involved tying off several small blood vessels. When Doctor Meadows said, "right", I was to release one of the artery forceps. We were progressing quite well and I was engrossed in my part of the procedure, when he said, "right." I released the clamp. A thin red stream shot up in the air about four feet. Immediately I snapped the clamp shut again, not before it had soaked the Doctor. After swabbing up the blood and wiping spots from his spectacles, he looked at me and said in a voice that he might have used to a disobedient child. "Why nurse, why?" You said, "right," sir, I gasped. It transpired that someone had signalled to him from the Theatre viewing window that there was a telephone call for him. He was replying to them. He then proceeded to inform the theatre staff in general, and me in particular, that as there were only 8 to 10 pints of blood in the average human body, nobody could afford to experiment with four foot jets of it.

Setting up a sterile trolley is a procedure for experts: so we were taught at PTS.(preliminary training school) where we spent three months before being let loose on the wards. It is a highly complicated procedure, the nurse, with the aid of a long forceps fishes the instruments and dishes out of the boiling steriliser. With smaller forceps, she delves into a container containing scalpels and surgical needles, selects the necessary items and transfers them to the trolley which she then covers with a sterile towel. If she drops anything, or if anyone touches anything in her hands while the trolley is being set up she must scrap it all and start again. Considering the fact that about 20 articles go in a sterile trolley including the covering cloths it would seem to be, indeed, a job for experts. Surprisingly enough, though, the technique is easily learned. The reader may imagine my concern when after only a week on the wards, I was required to set up such a trolley. There is a definite knack to handling cheatle forceps, the long 'fishing forceps' which I had not yet acquired. Painstakingly I struggled with the hot metal dishes and unfamiliar instruments and eventually it was finished. I had dreams of being congratulated on an excellent trolley and of being asked to witness the procedure for which it was to be used. Instead, the Staff Nurse gave a perfunctory glance, "not bad," she grunted, "now dismantle it, I just wanted to see if you knew how to lay up a trolley." I later learned that the words 'not bad' are quite high praise in hospital circles, where no one is over enthusiastic.

There is a certain incident concerning trolleys that I recall with shame even to this day. It happened on a busy radiotherapy ward when I was senior nurse on duty. We had two patients requiring blood transfusions, one who was having a lung aspirated, and no end of patients waiting to be admitted to the ward. I was setting up the blood transfusion trolley and, in order to be quick I emptied the contents of the previous trolley into the boiling steriliser without first sorting them out and washing them. It so happened that one of the gallipots was full of glycerine. I had to completely empty the steriliser and wash it out with soda, wash all the metal dishes, refill it and wait for it to boil again. Needless to say, I was in disgrace and the work piled up while I was sorting out my mistake. Since then I have insisted that every trolley must be dismantled correctly. Sister informed me that I was no more use than a ward maid, and unhappily, I had to agree with her on that occasion.

One hears much about the old type Ward Sister or Matron, the tyrannical type who has to be right every time. I only ever met one of that type, but she remains in my memory, one of my less pleasant memories. A colleague of mine was setting up a sterile trolley. The steriliser had just been filled and it was over the danger mark. My colleague badly scalded her finger, and when she went to have it dressed Sister Powell asked how it had happened. When told, her acid remark was, "well, you realise, nurse, that you have desterilised everything in the water." That was all the sympathy she got.

One of the Sisters on the radiotherapy block was considered to be a little eccentric. She was a vegetarian, and was always extolling the virtues of good green cabbage. Mr Yeoman was a market gardener, and in order to curry favour, he offered to supply the ward with a dinner of home grown vegetables. Sister Bowman jumped at the chance and later in the day baskets of carrots, spring onions, cabbages and potatoes arrived at the ward door. The ward kitchen had no facilities for cooking, the catering was done in the large basement kitchen, and so one of the nurses was detailed to carry the baskets downstairs. On the stairs she met the Administrative Sister, and, not knowing if the office staff would condone individual cooking for a ward, Nurse Graham hid the basket behind her back. This proved quite difficult as it was heavy and cumbersome. The Admin Sister appeared not to notice anything unusual, though, I suspect it was a similar situation to when Nelson placed his telescope to his blind eye.

There are periodical attacks of insanity among student nurses and one of these took the form of the 'ghostie' craze. Everywhere one went in the hospital they were confronted by little drawings of a heap with two holes for eyes, and underneath was written 'ghostie'. Unexpectedly, at bends in the corridor, one would bump into some object covered with a sheet, and labelled 'ghostie'. They even found their way into the patient's notes and confidential files. No one knew how they got there, and like so many other crazes, they just disappeared with time. One day when this craze was at its height, and no one important was on duty, I donned a sheet and glided into Male Surgical Ward. The patients froze when a voice just behind me said, "infection, nurse." It hadn't occurred to me that by dressing up in a sheet out of the dirty laundry bin I was shaking micro organisms over a 20 yard radius. The Houseman had just come to do a round of his patients.

Another craze that hit the hospital at about the same time was the woolly toy craze. Everyone started frantically knitting woollen bears and cats and rabbits. Matron stopped to admire a collection of these on a patient's locker. She picked up a rabbit and turned it round, and there, protruding from its tail she found - yes, you've guessed it - hospital cotton wool. Not even the grey wool used for sluicing, but the pure white expensive kind. Matron didn't remark on this fact, but the next day on the notice board there was something to the effect that economy with government property was advised. Thus died the woolly toy craze.

Some of the answers in nurses exam papers are enlightening, to say the least. The dermatologist at my training hospital had a reputation for sarcasm. One of the questions in our dermatology paper was, 'describe the principal features and treatment of eczema'. Nurse Garret was an excellent practical nurse but she had great difficulty in expressing herself on paper.

A feature of eczema is that the skin tends to go scaly at first, then it suppurates. Nurse Garret's answer paper read thus: The skin breaks down and weeps. To her way of thinking was quite correct, but the answer paper came back with a little drawing of a hand, with a face drawn on the palm and tears running from its eyes, and underneath, a question mark. It had always been drummed into the nurses that ordinary lay terms are not used in hospital life. 'It's not a common cold, nurse, it's chorysa,' or 'it's not a nose bleed, it's epistaxis.' This caused difficulty sometimes because one of the doctors who, incidentally, always sided with the student nurses, would try to simplify his lectures so that we would understand them better. When talking about bronchitis, he would say that patients tended to have acute flare ups of the disease. Naturally, that was the term we used in our answer papers, and the next day Sister tutor gave us a long lecture on the merits of using medical terms as opposed to, 'acute flare ups'.

Old people often have difficulty in adjusting to hospital life. Sometimes the psychological change is so great that for a few days they become completely disorientated. They imagine themselves to be anywhere except in hospital, and sometimes can become almost violent. Mr Griffiths was admitted at 5am after having fallen down a flight of stairs. He had apparently lain unconscious all night and the cleaning lady found him. He was admitted to Casualty in a sorry state. There were numerous cuts and bruises all over his body, and he had a fractured femur. For the first day he was quiet and seemed to be anxiously looking around but when evening came he grew more and more agitated. Eventually he was bellowing at the top of his voice and struggling to get the traction off his leg. If anyone came within throwing distance he would hurl the contents of his locker at them, all the time shouting abuse. Nurses are not usually prudes, but his language would have made an Irish navvy green with envy.

Harry Thomas was a colourful character. He had been a seaman in his youth and had travelled the world, incidentally acquiring some unusual tattoos en route. He had finished up as a vagrant, tramping the West Country. He was brought into casualty one night suffering from exposure and head injuries. A policeman on the beat had found him unconscious behind a picture hoarding. We assumed he had been beaten up and left there. Harry was said to be suffering from amnesia but, from conversations I had with him, I suspected that it wasn't total amnesia. When the burly, heavy footed constable came to visit him, he would remember nothing and assume a bewildered look. "Huh," he remarked when the policeman had gone, "coppers and quacks is all the same, can't mind their own business. I'll get them as done me without no 'elp from 'im."

Sholto Johnson was a huge West Indian. We admitted him one evening suffering from the accumulated after effects of riotous living. He was plagued not only by delirium tremens, but had rampant syphilis, to boot. There were three women who used to visit him, each calling herself Mrs Johnson. Sholto was quite unperturbed, and never seemed unduly worried by the possibility of their visits coinciding. For some weeks things went smoothly when the inevitable happened and the three of them arrived at once. We were idling away in the sluice, when Nurse Evans rushed in shouting. "It's happened, it's happened." "for heavens sake," I shouted, "what's happened?" "They've come together, all three of them, Sholto's people," she grinned. "Look here, let's take it in relays to stroll down the ward and see what goes on." So for the next hour we kept each other informed about progress in the ward. It was a bit disappointing really. There was no big scene as we had expected, but after that we only saw one Mrs Johnson at visiting time.

A strict code of etiquette is observed during training, certain things are just not done, for example, a first year nurse addressing a consultant surgeon. Nurse Callaghan discovered this the hard way. We were frantic on Miller Ward. The beds had been pulled out ready to dust and the orderly was sluggishly pushing a broom along. Staff nurse Davies was snapping at everybody, impatient to get dressings started and Sister bell was sniffing around in the hope of finding something done badly or some dust where there shouldn't be any. Mr Pirie stood at the entrance to the long ward, apparently surveying the scene. Young Nurse Callaghan, ever ready to please rushed up and asked him who he wanted to see. "Could I see Sister please," he enquired. She asked him to wait on a bench in the corridor and went in search of Sister. "Please Sister," she began. "Away with you girl, can't you see I'm busy." Sister snapped. "But" "Now listen to me, nurse. I have neither the time nor the inclination to chat to you, go and see Staff nurse." Callaghan scuttled away and went in search of Staff Nurse, only to receive a similar reception. Deflated, she went to tell the gentleman in the corridor that Sister was busy, but on the way was so inundated with requests for Mrs Jones's milk drink, and a bedpan for Miss Farley, that she completely forgot her original errand. Twenty minutes later, Sister found the Senior Consultant Surgeon patiently waiting on the bench in the corridor. He had been ordered to sit and wait, he told her. Luckily, he was a sport, and didn't say who told him to wait or how long he had been waiting.

Mr Ross had been on Monroe Ward for months, and knew all the ward routine like the back of his hand. He knew every patient and their complaints, the times for special feeds or treatments. In short, he was the ward's general factotum. He had been brought in with severe burns when a cauldron of molten metal had exploded at his factory. Sister Bell and her team had nursed him back from the brink of death, and he had undergone several painful skin grafts and weeks of suspense lying on his back waiting to see if they would take. All this was now behind him and he was well on the road to recovery. The doctors were justly proud of the result of their painstaking labours, and exhibited Mr Ross whenever possible. So much so, that he began to think he was the only patient that mattered. He would wake up at 3 am and demand a cup of tea, or, alternatively, wait until the visitors were clamouring at the ward door and ask for his back to be rubbed. This involved bringing out the screens and delaying the visitors. He was kindhearted, though, and tried to be helpful in his pottering way.

Chapter 3

Psychiatry is an extremely interesting and nowadays, quite a rewarding field. To see a sullen, insecure and unhappy person change in a matter of weeks to a normal, lively and friendly young woman is in itself reward enough for all the rigours of psychiatric nursing. With the newest treatment and drugs, psychiatric illness is no longer a thing to be feared. Whereas, forty years ago anyone with the slightest hint of mental instability could expect nothing better than to be locked away in an 'institution' never again to live a normal life. Not only that, but their families would carry the stigma, too. Today these people can be helped tremendously without ever having to set foot inside a psychiatric hospital. I recall nursing one dear old gentleman at a hospital for mental and nervous disorders. He would appear every morning for occupational therapy, meticulously dressed in a suit, neatly pressed, white handkerchief at his breast pocket, sedate tie at his neck but no shirt. I never found out why he did this. He could hold intelligent conversation with anyone and indeed, the only thing that separated him from other so called normal people was the absence of a shirt. After three months at this hospital I began to wonder just where the dividing line lay between sanity and psychosis. The patients there, for the most part, spoke, thought and acted as I did myself. Indeed, it was only on close inspection and intensive questioning that one could perceive anything wrong. But, as I have already stated, medicine has made such tremendous advances in the last forty years, and twenty more years from now, who knows? I leave it with the reader.

The nurse comes up against some pathetic situations occasionally. I remember when I was nursing at a hospital for infectious diseases, there was an old gentleman with tuberculosis. He had been with us for some months and was cured. He played the banjo and every evening it came to be the accepted thing that all the nurses would gather round his bed and have a little sing song. We would go through all the old George Formby songs and as few modern ones, too. This came to be a part of ward life that we really looked forward to. The old man revelled in the happiness he gave to us and the other patients. One day, coming on duty, I found him very downcast. It appeared that he had been declared fit and could return home. He was fully cured. The pathetic thing was he had no family or friends, and was going back to one room, with only his old age pension. We had really grown to love this old man, and he us. Of course, he was technically fit for discharge so nothing could be done. We sadly missed him, and I believe some of my colleagues still visit him occasionally.

The problem of old folk with nowhere to go for affection and company is very real. The hospital almoners do marvels in this field, and if ever there was a job more difficult yet more rich in reward, it is theirs. In the same ward as the old man mentioned previously, there was an inmate of one of her Majesty's prisons. He had contracted tuberculosis while a guest of the Queen and had been transferred to our hospital. He was a really likeable character, and did all he could to help us and the other patients. He had only six months of his sentence to serve, and although he was cured and should have gone back to prison for the rest of his sentence, he was such a genuinely nice chap that doctors and administrative staff alike conspired to keep him in a while longer. Of course, Joe had nothing to lose and everything to gain by staying with us. The prison authorities began to smell a rat, and towards the end of his six months there were several visits from prison doctors and such like people. Our doctors, bless their crooked hearts, stuck to their guns and Joe walked out of hospital a free man.

As the nurse gains more experience she begins to notice certain dominant characteristics about people. Tenacity, for example. This brings to mind the case of Mrs Jones. She had to have her left leg amputated below the knee because of a wasting disease of the bone. One of her relatives was sorting out her locker for her and discarding the accumulation of papers and rubbish. The relative came across Mrs Jones's left slipper, one of an old and worn looking pair, and placed it in the waste bin. At that moment the Ward Sister came in and saw it. She was very annoyed indeed and took the relative outside to talk to her. At the time I remember thinking Sister was a bit unjust, after all, Mrs Jones wouldn't be needing her left slipper again. This just goes to show the extent of my inexperience with people. Two years later, I met a woman in the shopping centre, she was smartly dressed, confident, and with a face I vaguely recognised. Only when she said, "hello nurse Jenkins," did I realise who she was. Involuntarily, I glanced downward. It took more than a cursory glance to notice the artificial leg. She had perfect control of it. I learned, too, that she still had those slippers, and wore them about the house. Seeing Mrs Jones with her artificial leg made me realise the psychological harm that was nearly done that day two years ago when her left slipper was almost thrown out. Yes, we live and learn, and that incident taught me much.

As the nurse passes through the first year she gains experience by doing the menial tasks and watching her older colleagues doing the difficult things. This is a fairly easy year in some respects, although there are the trials of homesickness and the feeling of being a nobody, the lowest of the low, in fact. The second year, however, is much different. I hated my second year of training. It is a kind of in between stage. The nurse has neither the innocence of the first year nor the authority of the third year. She is expected to still do many of the menial tasks of the first year, but to perform them perfectly, and, on the other hand she is expected to do some quite difficult procedures efficiently. This, I think is the moulding stage where she gradually learns to accept responsibility. What is not so pleasant is the fact that the second year nurse comes in for all the criticism of everyone. The juniors know no better anyway, and the seniors can always manage to pass the buck, so the second year nurse gets it all ways. All things considered, not a very pleasant year in training for State Registration. The third year of training was the one I really enjoyed. There was the confidence the extra stripe on my cap afforded, The little privileges of having coffee in Sisters office, or the Houseman consulting me on which medication to give Mrs Edwards. Also, by the third year of training the nurse gets accustomed to homesickness, she makes friends in the nurses home, or if she is living out in a flat there is the added independence. There is more money, which is an important factor when one has struggled to make ends meet for two years. Also there is the self confidence that comes with efficiency. And efficiency does come, believe it or not. There is the excitement and apprehension of state finals in the near future. All things considered, there is no standing still in the third year. Everything moves at a rapid pace to the conclusion - that is - a little badge with State Registered Nurse and your name engraved on it. A highly coveted possession. (in the forty odd years since first writing this, the badge has ceased to exist)

One of the things a senior nurse has to learn is the technique of handling junior nurses, and correcting their mistakes in such a way that they do not go in tears to the Ward Sister, or rebel and do the exact opposite of what she says. Tact is a necessary quality in a senior nurse, and there was one particular incident when my tact was tested to the full. It was a bitterly cold day in the middle of February, and Mrs Jacobs was asking for a bed pan, indeed, she had been asking for twenty minutes. I drew the attention of the junior to this, and said, "don't forget to warm it, will you." Anyone who has had an Ice cold bedpan thrust under them will appreciate that remark. Little nurse Redmond was gone some time, and Mrs Jacobs was getting desperate.   Eventually I was forced to go and investigate. There was Nurse Redmond, warming the bed pan as instructed, but over the flame of a Bunsen burner. The usual procedure is to hold it under a warm tap just to take the chill off.

There are times in the third year when the nurse is in danger of becoming over confident. Maybe things have been progressing very well for some months and she has been coping efficiently with all the problems that come her way.   I had reached this happy state just before final exams and the little incident that I am about to relate brought me back to earth sharply.   As there was no junior nurse available I was asked to escort an unconscious patient back to the Ward after a laparoscopy. We had reached the Ward, and I had got her into bed when I noticed the tell tale bluish tinge to her skin denoting some degree of asphyxia. Promptly I started artificial respiration. There was no response whatsoever. After a few seconds no pulse was perceptible and she had assumed an extreme pallor. The ward nurse was standing by and I hissed. "Quick, fetch somebody." The Houseman was in the adjoining ward and he came immediately. He gave the girl a hearty thump between her shoulder blades and began more artificial respiration. This time it revived the patient. Afterwards he explained to me that she had vomited, and breathed some of it into her bronchial tubes. The thump had dislodged the secretions and cleared the lungs for artificial respiration. It was divine providence that sent that Houseman along at the right time because she had actually stopped breathing when he arrived.

I once spent time in a hospital for victims of poliomyelitis, or infantile paralysis, as it used to be called. There was every kind of breathing apparatus there from the gigantic 'iron lung' to the portable

Clifton bellows apparatus. To see some of these polio victims was an education in itself. Never have I seen such courage and grim determination to conquer the effects of the disease. It is humbling to see people afflicted, as these were and yet as cheerful as if there were no crippling afflictions in every joint of their bodies. One woman I think of in particular, Mrs George, she was a woman with a growing family when poliomyelitis stuck her down at the age of 34. She was completely paralysed, and all she could move was her tongue, yet she devised a way of communication that we all grew to understand. If she wanted something she would push out her tongue, and when we came we would go through the alphabet until we came to the letters that spelled the thing she wanted. She would put out her tongue when we reached the right word, and thus she spelled messages to us and to her family. Someone had to keep a special watch on her, day and night because she was in an iron lung and if the mechanism failed once it would prove fatal. Thus it was that Mrs George got to know us very well indeed, we really grew to admire her for her courage and cheerfulness.

There was another young man in the same hospital. He could only move his fingers and neck muscles. One of the doctors had an engineering degree as well as his medical qualifications and he designed a chair for Mr McKensie. It was a complicated piece of machinery, and by pressing buttons placed at his fingertips, Mr McKenzie could go all around the grounds of the hospital in this chair. He had so developed the muscles in his neck that he had no need of an artificial respirator in the day time but breathed by lifting his head and taking in gulps of air. At first this was disconcerting, but we soon grew accustomed to seeing this and hardly noticed it eventually. Only when he went to bed did he have a respirator. An outsider may be tempted to wonder why these people kept such great spirit in the face of such difficulties. I think the answer lies in what the doctor attending these patients told us in a lecture once. He said that with the frontiers of medicine growing wider every day, and so many breathtaking new discoveries being made almost hourly, who knows that tomorrow someone may not come out with a revolutionary new drug to treat and cure paralytic poliomyelitis. These people, quite literally, are living in hope. (bear in mind, this was written long before there was an effective vaccine readily available).

During the three years one of the things a nurse learns is not to show any emotion such as shock, panic or fear. She may feel it, in fact she often does, but it does untold harm to show a patient her negative feelings. A patient tends to put his trust in the medical staff, and often when in his heart he knows the worst, he looks to them for a calmness that helps him to accept many things.

I was on Women's Medical Ward and we were frantically busy one morning. We had the usual run of ladies wanting bedpans quickly, one or two new patients to be admitted and charts to be maintained. There was one patient who needed constant monitoring and one who was in a coma. All this, apart from the usual routine ward work. Mrs Rogers, the grand old lady of the ward was sitting up in bed with headphones listening to the radio. Suddenly she shouted across the ward, "where's the little Welsh nurse." I came over and she told me that there was something in the news about my home town. I stole a moment to listen in, and it was with a sickening feeling of horror that I heard what was being said. There had been an explosion underground in the little mining town where I lived, and many men were trapped in the pit. Rescue workers were digging their way through. There were about 50 men underground. I knew that my father would have been finishing the night shift at 7am. But there was no mention of the time that the explosion occurred. There were many seriously ill patients on the ward and there simply wasn't time to make a long distance phone call. I just had to endure the mental anguish of not knowing anything until my coffee break, which was an hour away. I will never know what sustained me in that hour. Maybe the shock was delayed, and my nervous system was unable to take in everything until later. When I was able to phone home I was reassured at least about my father. Many childhood friends and neighbours had been killed. It was a terrible disaster. There were only two survivors. I believe all the patients shared in my anxiety, and felt too, my relief to know that this tragedy had passed by my own family. Personal grief and feelings have no place in nursing sick people, but those patients were a comfort to me that day.

I reported for duty one evening after seeing my fiancé. He was leaving to catch a coach back to Lincolnshire. I was on Casualty at the time, and I had been working for about half an hour when the phone rang. It was the doctor to say we were admitting a casualty from a road accident. As I took down the particulars, I realised that the patient had the same name and age as my fiancé. After the initial shock I started conjuring up visions of playing the ministering angel to him, cool hands on fevered brows and all that. I had just about persuaded myself that it was bound to be John. As it happened, I was wrong. The same name and age but an entirely different person. I was glad, of course, but I must confess, I wondered what kind of patient he would have made. Now, after over 40 years of marriage, I know!

A Saturday night in the Casualty department of any large teaching hospital is likely to be eventful. On average there are about ten to fifteen men in various stages of intoxication, ranging from high spirits to downright pugnaciousness. As well there are the usual run of splinters in feet, nosebleeds, broken limbs, foreign bodies and road accidents. One such Saturday night we were so busy there was hardly time to breath, when in marched an unusual procession. First, there was a large swarthy Spaniard, followed by a frail coffee coloured woman, her blue black hair all in disarray. She was leading by the hand a small, scrawny figure with his hand stuck firmly in the top of an expensive looking porcelain vase. Neither of these people spoke English and there was general pandemonium when we tried to remove the vase. As it looked expensive we were reluctant to break it. Eventually we half filled it with olive oil and somehow the lad managed to wriggle free. On another occasion we were called upon to remove a man's finger from the hole for paper money in a child's piggy bank. This proved extremely difficult as the finger had swollen to twice its normal size.

There is usually a friendly atmosphere on the convalescent wards. The patients are so glad to be finished with operations and on the road to recovery, they have a certain sense of well being now that the actual operation is behind them. They form a comradeship with their fellow patients due, partly to sharing the same experiences. We witnessed the growth of a firm friendship between a vicar's wife and a prostitute on one occasion. Neither of these knew the others situation. Maybe, if they had the unseen social barriers would have gone up and prevented any contact between them. Much of the loneliness experienced by young mothers who have had to give up working in a crowded office to sit at home with an uncommunicative baby need never arise. If people could learn to take their neighbours as they find them, to offer help occasionally and not to be put off because they seem to be always busy with children. Most wives and mothers long for adult company. There are few things more uninspiring to an intelligent young woman than to have no better mental stimulation from 9 am till 5pm than the conversation of two and three year olds, however adorable they may be.

Loneliness can take many different forms, ranging from the desperate, cut off feeling of the adolescent. He feels that no one has ever had to face such a turmoil of warring emotions as himself. At the other end of the scale to the old age pensioner, whose family have all grown up and married, and, widowed, he sits alone day after day with hardly a ring at the door bell. The nurse learns to recognise the outward signs of loneliness. There is the patient who reaches for her hand as she rushes down the ward. This patient just wants the comfort of a friendly word and a smile, or just the sheer pleasure of having someone to talk to.

There is the man who sits up in bed and loudly airs his views on politics and current events. Just another manifestation of loneliness. Reader, if you are contemplating a career in nursing, learn to recognise and most important, sympathise with, the lonely patient. Many small points like this make the difference between a nurse and a mere bed pan carrier.

There was an elderly spinster on my ward, and every time the opportunity arose she would stop and tell me all about her husband. He was, of course, non existent. She would tell me at great length how good he was, and what he brought her each visiting time and how he had to work sometimes and couldn't come and see her. She was a dear old soul and no one ever questioned her about her ringless finger, and the type written 'miss' on her documents. Evidently, this husband was an image conjured up to combat the awful loneliness of an unmarried elderly woman, desperately ill, and approaching the end of her life.

The nurse sees much of sickness and death. Many times in the last moments of a patient's life, he will reach out, seemingly for some human contact. The need for a human presence at such times, a familiar face and a calm bearing must be great. It is a privilege to be with the Christian patient at such a time. There is no fear, just a quiet confidence. They have a strong belief that no matter how Jordans waters heave and toss. He is on the other bank with His arms stretched out to them.

Chapter 4

The effects of a long period of duty on the Radiotherapy Ward was always a subject for discussion in the common room. Sister Morton, or Sterile Beryl, as she was called had been on Radiotherapy for as long as anyone could remember, but as she was a dyed in the wool spinster, nobody ever questioned the effects of the ward on her reproductive system. My name was on the notice board to change wards on Sunday. It was with much speculation that I walked into the ward on Sunday morning. I was greeted with a cool look from Sterile Beryl. "Hmph, so you're Nurse Jenkins, go and see to Mrs Everards dressing and don't contaminate yourself." Bewildered, I went in search of Mrs Everard. She was a quaint old lady in an old fashioned lace fronted nightie, her hair done in two long grey plaits. I uncovered the dressing gingerly, not quite knowing what I would find underneath. She had had radium needles implanted into a malignant growth, and the skin had broken down. The wound was wet and needed cleaning with eusol. I proceeded to clean and dress it. Mrs Everard gripped my sleeve and said plaintively, "Why do you do it, dear?" "It's my job." I replied. "Oh, such a pity, you looks a nice wee thing, too." I didn't take much notice of what she was saying until she said in a warning tone, "sooner or later the police'll come then you'll have to let me go, there's a place for girls like you." I stared at her aghast, wondering what on earth she was talking about. She took on a stubborn look and would say no more, only glowered at me. I learned afterwards that Mrs Everard thought she was being kept prisoner in a brothel. This was one of her milder periods, sometimes she got almost unmanageable and had to be given tranquilising injections.

There were half a dozen patients on Lewis Ward with thyrotoxicosis. This is a condition where the whole metabolism is speeded up. The thyroid gland is secreting too much thyroid hormone and it affects the whole character and personality of the patient. Thyrotoxic patients are usually very restless, quick and jerky in their movements and often irritable. They are characteristically thin although they consume tremendous quantities of food. With six such women on Lewis ward the tempo was considerably increased. If they wanted anything, they wanted it at once, their temperament did not allow for waiting. They were all having radio active isotope treatment and were kept in a special, 'ward within a ward.' They virtually breathed radio active air, and had to have special crockery and bedding. Every time they used a bedpan it had to be emptied into a special container and tested with a Geiger counter. One busy morning Nurse Webb tripped while carrying a bedpan full of radio active urine and spread the contents all the length of the cubicle. She tramped up to Sister's office to confess her crime and left a trail of radio active footprints. It was months before Nurse Webb was able to forget the incident, and for ages after, her shoes were out on the verandah getting rid of the radiation.

It was the habit of girls coming off duty to check themselves with Geiger counters to see how much radioactivity they had picked up during the day. In spite of all the precautions we took, most of us registered some. There were never any after effects that we could see.

One of the patients, Mrs Moore, professed the ability to see into the future. When we were not busy we would gather round her bed and she would tell our fortunes. She could only tell a limited number at a time because of, "me vibrations, duckie." She claimed to be able to feel vibrations coming from the nurse whose fortune she was telling. She was in the middle of telling me that I would have a house and three children, when a vinegary voice broke in. "That may be your distant future, Nurse Jenkins, but your immediate future is to go and attend to Mrs Everard's dressing." After that we were all summoned to Sister's office and lectured on the things that were beneath the dignity of a nurse, and certainly not ethical.

Mrs Chester was the grand old lady of Harper Ward, she was bordering on ninety-four years of age. Whereas she had once kept the ward amused with her banter, she was now growing daily more feeble. She hardly had the strength to complain about the nurses, and that, in such a patient as Mrs Chester, was a bad sign. We were cutting up dressings in the treatment room one Sunday when Nurse Morley came rushing in to say that she thought Granny Chester had swallowed her false teeth. We all rushed to see what could be done. There was Granny, propped up on pillows, looking quite self satisfied, and minus her top set of dentures. The portable X ray machine was sent for, and the Houseman alerted in Theatre. The X ray plate was negative. We searched her locker, the bed, her handbag and everywhere else we could think of, but no sign of the elusive top set. For days we hunted, everyone was asked, but no one had seen them. Gradually, the interest died down, then, on the following Saturday they were returned with the laundry together with a pert note. "Would Sister please address some biting remarks to the nurse responsible." Needless to say, Sister did. There are many weird and wonderful things that find their way to the hospital laundry, including spectacles, money, a glass eye and tablets of all kinds.

Harper Ward was always a hive of activity, there were usually five or six patients admitted for operations as well as the few seriously ill patients needing special attention. One Monday morning when the Theatre list unusually long, the telephone started ringing. Nurse Mead, the junior at that time answered. It was someone asking for Miss Stone, she was one of the patients who had just been taken to Theatre. The person enquiring began to get rather irate. It turned out that Miss Stone, as well as being one of the patients scheduled for operation, was also the name of the new Registrar. Nurse Mead had apparently told the medical secretary that Miss Stone had just been wheeled out of the ward on a trolley.

Lucas King Ward was renowned throughout the hospital. It was the Male Convalescent Ward. The men were not well enough to go home, but quite well enough to stay up all day and potter about. They were usually a very high spirited crowd and the nurse on duty always had a lively time trying to keep some kind of order. Johnny Marks, a young docker was convalescing after an accident.

He was the life and soul of the ward. It was not unusual for the nurse to arrive on the ward and find Johnny prancing up the middle of the ward in pyjama trousers doing an imitation of Maria Pavlova. He was brought back to earth with a bump the day he decided to make a snake out of rubber tubing and put it in Fred Thomas's bed. Fred was a highly strung, squeaky voiced boy, and came in for a lot of good natured teasing from the other men on the ward. He had just come back from a walk in the grounds, when he pulled back the sheets and there, just by his pillow, was a slimy long green thing. Fred's reaction was alarming. He stood petrified for a few seconds, then let out a terrified yelp and ran right down the ward, falling in a dead faint by the desk just as Matron decided to do a round. Of course, there was a great to do and the hospital governors got to know about it. A notice was posted up to the effect that all treatment room equipment was to be locked up and the key to be kept in possession of a trained nurse. Hence, every time we overworked nurses wanted so much as a sticking plaster, we had to hunt out Sister for the key. That wasn't the end of the story, for weeks afterwards, poor Fred would wake up sweating and shouting. Johnny was really ashamed and was observed to be much quieter after this.

When you are in charge of a ward, if only for a few hours, It is something of a responsibility. This was brought home to me while I was on night duty. I had been sent to Frazer Ward to relieve the Senior nurse. It was deadly quiet, there was no sound at all except the even breathing of about 30 women. I strolled up the ward to make sure that everyone was asleep and comfortable. On the way back to the desk I glanced out of the window, and there on the balcony was a man with a shotgun. My first reaction, strangely enough, was surprise, panic came about four seconds later. The decision I had to make was whether to go back and phone the porters lodge, and risk this burglar breaking into the ward, or at least to have one of my patients wake up and see him and have hysterics. I decided to be brave and tell him to go away. Almost automatically, I acted. Opening the French window I put my head out and in my most authoritative voice, I said.

"What do you think you are doing?" "It's all right, love," came the reply, "I'm shooting the pigeons with matron's permission." He was telling the truth, too. The pigeons had been a bit of a nuisance, nesting around the ward, and the hospital management committee had decided to liquidate them. The gun was fitted with a silencer so as not to disturb the patients. Apparently, every night nurse in the hospital had been informed except me. Night Sister thought it was all very amusing.

Contrary to popular belief, not many nurses manage to hook a doctor for a husband. There is generally quite keen competition for the attentions of the unattached male members of staff. It's easy to discern the cause of some of the catty remarks - such remarks as. "Oh, I see it's your turn tonight, he took me dancing last week," or, "I see that engagement ring is on your finger now, it's certainly done the rounds." Sister Harry and nurse Anstey were both head over heels in love with John Waltham, a young house surgeon. As Mary Anstey worked on Sister Harry's ward, she had a rough time of it. Old Harry, as she was called would find any excuse to make Mary work later than her duty hours, and if anything went wrong on the ward, it was Mary who got the blame. She triumphed in the end, though, because she gave up her training and married Dr Waltham. The patients were particularly pleased about this. There is a kind of grapevine in hospital wards. Patients who have little to do except observe the nurses, become sensitive to all the little changes of atmosphere on the ward. They can tell at once if Nurse Evans has broken off her engagement again, or if Ruby, the ward maid is still on speaking terms with her husband. Petty trivialities, maybe, but when you are on your back for weeks on end, study of human nature and events around you can become extremely interesting. Staff Nurse Meyrick was newly married and just back from her honeymoon. She bustled around all day humming, and had a bright beaming smile for everyone. One morning Nurse Evans found her in tears in the sluice. "Why, Staff, whatever is the matter?" "It's my wedding ring," she sobbed, "I've broken a thermometer and the mercury has turned it silver in patches." This was indeed a catastrophe, no one knew of any chemical that would remove the mercury without harming the gold. Staff Nurse was getting more and more upset. We went down to dispensary but no one knew of anything there. By some stroke of good fortune I bumped into the Professor of Pathology. "Excuse me sir," I began hesitantly and went on to explain the situation to him. "Ah, dilute nitric acid," he exclaimed. Staff Nurse was summoned to the Pathology Laboratory where the professor proceeded to remove the mercury. She didn't want to take the ring from her finger at first, but when he showed her what acid could do to a piece of wood she changed her mind.

A typical diabetic patient is often fat, fair and fortyish. So said Mr Brownlow in one of his lectures. Mrs Williams fitted that description aptly, she had been in regularly to have her diabetes stabilised with regular blood monitoring and doses of insulin, but in between whiles she would not stick to her diet. She craved sweet things, and had twice been brought in on the point of death in a hyperglycaemic coma, caused by indulging this craving. For some days the routine tests had shown a high sugar content in her urine. The dose of insulin was increased but with little effect. That afternoon I discovered the reason. I was doing a last minute tidying of the ward before Matron's round, and noticed some sweet wrappers underneath Mrs Williams' bed. She denied all knowledge of them and swore that it must have been Mrs Davies in the opposite bed. I picked up a pile of magazines from her bed and put them in her locker to be tidy for the round, at the same time taking a surreptitious peep inside. Sure enough, there they were, a whole packet of mint creams. There was such a guilty look on her face that I realised she knew her secret was out. Strangely enough, from then on her tests became more and more normal. She was able to be discharged the following week. While clearing out her locker after her discharge, I came across the same packet of mint creams, presumably left for the nurses. An unspoken promise to stick to her diet, I presumed.

Sister Jameson was one of those people who remain always in the memory. Once you had worked with her and put up with her eccentric ways you remembered her for life. If the ward was ever short of a nurse, whereas other Sisters would ask for extra help and wait patiently until it came although it may take a week, Jamie would storm up to Matron's office and demand a nurse at once. "Never mind where you get her from, I need a nurse." She always got one, too, I think even Matron was a little bit afraid of her. She adored the patients, and would willingly stay on duty hours overtime to see that they were comfortable. She had been known to stay on day and night when a little boy was seriously ill. Woe betide any nurse she took a dislike to, though. She could, and invariably would, make their working life a misery. Jamie detested abbreviations and insisted that all reports be written correctly and nothing cut down. If a new nurse made the mistake of writing PDU in the report book, instead of perforated duodenal ulcer, she would yell at the nurse down the length of the ward, and her language was not always professional. Terry Greaves was admitted via Casualty with a piece of metal filing embedded in his eye. He was clutching a single piece of paper which displayed the following information. Greaves T. age 29. FB in L eye. Please admit. Jamie read the paper, reached for the phone and bellowed down the line. "Tell the BF in casualty, we've admitted the foreign body, and would he come up and remove it."

A situation every nurse thinks of with delight is to have a Sister as a patient. When we heard that Sister Evans from Everton Ward was coming in with a slipped disc, speculation ran high as to the kind of treatment she would receive. Mary Morris, a nurse well known for her rather rude manner to private patients, aired her views loudly in her lilting Welsh accent. "Stuff her pillow with horse hair, I will, hammer 6 inch nails in her bed boards."

Sister Evans made a much better patient than a Sister. She was considerate and never rang her bell unnecessarily. We all felt ashamed of the way we had thought to treat her. Even so, we still had the feeling she was summing up our efficiency.

Old Sister Wilkes had been on Harper Ward for more than thirty years, she must have been near to retiring age but nobody dared mention it. She had her own methods for treating the patients and although they were considered to be years out of date they were always effective. As a student nurse, fresh from preliminary training school, I was asked to do the dressings on Harper Ward. The trolley I set up was ultra modern, the latest method was swabbing the glass with chlorhexidine in spirit, instead of a sterile towel, one of a few new fangled ideas from our newly qualified clinical instructor. Sister Wilkes glanced at the trolley when it was ready. "Haven't you got that trolley laid up yet, nurse?" she demanded. Hesitantly, I explained that this was the latest technique for laying up a sterile trolley. She glared at me and called for Staff Nurse Whelan. "Show this nurse how things should be done on my ward, Staff Nurse," she snapped. Bridey Whelan tried to explain to me while we reset the trolley. On this ward, sweetie, there is no technique except the Wilkes technique, thirty years old it may be, but it's her ward." I was afterwards to discover that she had had three assistant sisters on the ward in the last few months and none of them would stay. The back rounds on Harper ward were never ending. Whereas the modern method was to simply turn the bedridden patients on alternate sides every two hours to prevent pressure sores, on Harper it was a different matter altogether. There was a special back trolley, containing soap, methylated spirits, powder, cotton wool and various other oddments. Every two hours the nurses would go round all the patients, wash their pressure areas with soap and water, rub the soap in vigorously until the skin was dry, rub methylated spirit in until it was dry again, and finish off with dusting powder. Sister Evan's backs were her pride and joy. At the slightest sign of redness anywhere she would personally inspect the patients back every two hours until the redness disappeared. I can never remember anyone on Harper Ward with pressure sores, and there were patients who had been paralysed and bedridden for months on end.

The day the junior set got their caps was a memorable one. We worked on the wards for three months without a cap, Then if Matron saw fit, we were given a plain white cap. On the morning in question, old Mrs Mayberry called me over and asked me to pop into town for her. "I want you to get two little presents, nursie, she said. "They're for two little girls about your age, just choose something you think would suit them." I rushed out in my dinner break and quickly purchased two rather pretty make up bags. That evening there was a parcel in my pigeon hole. Opening it, I found one of the make up bags with a little note - congratulations on reaching your cap stage, Mrs Mayberry. I checked with the other nurse from our set on Harper Ward, she too had received one. We were more thrilled with that little gift than with our new starchy caps.

Sister Evans was notoriously careless with the bunch of ward keys. They were liable to be found almost anywhere on the ward. She would say despairingly, "run and get the keys for me, Nurse, they're on the office table, and if they're not there try the kitchen." More often than not they would be in the sluice or by the hall telephone. Nurse Mountford took advantage of this carelessness to have a clay mold made of Sister's personal cupboard key. Her stocks of coffee and sugar kept mysteriously diminishing, and, although she never complained she almost certainly suspected something. One morning she called Nurse Mountford into her office. "If you must break the rules and have coffee on the ward, nurse, kindly remove your dirty cup from under my desk." Carol Mountford had been having a quiet cup of coffee the night before when she had been surprised by the Senior Night Sister and had just managed to hide the cup in time.

On the whole, children make easy patients except when there is one high spirited child in the ward, and then nursing them becomes an impossibility. Mary was eleven years old, and the best that can be said for her was that she was a natural leader. No matter what mischief was going on in the ward, Mary was at the forefront. If the nurse went to the desk drawer and found it full of rubbish from the wastepaper bin, Mary was involved somehow. If a book fell on her head as she opened the ward door, Mary's merry laugh would ring out. Nurse Bayliss put up with all this patiently but the day when she walked into the ward to be soaked with water from sterile syringes manned by

Mary and co. Cynthia Bayliss put her foot down. After ordering all the children to bed she stamped off to Sister's office to ask to be moved somewhere peaceful, like Male Convalescent.

The daughter of a high up hospital official was admitted to Children's Ward for a tonsillectomy. A more odious child it would be hard to find. If the nurse pressed her to eat she would tell daddy, "The food is terrible." If the nurse made any little mistakes on the ward she would save them up to tell 'Daddy'. The day I nearly gave her the wrong medicine stands out in my memory. She waited until her parents came and blurted out a much exaggerated account of what had happened. "It could have killed me, Daddy," I heard as I passed her bed. Of course, the outraged parents wanted to know the why and wherefore of it all, and I ended up on the carpet in Matron's office. "I am sadly disappointed in you, nurse." We were not in the least bit surprised when 'darling Angela' had complications after her tonsillectomy. I am convinced that it was fate's way of making us keep her in longer. I was on duty alone the evening she came back from Theatre, with no one within calling distance. She just bled and bled, and it seemed nothing I could do had any effect. As she wasn't fully conscious I couldn't leave her to phone for help. Eventually one of the Housemen popped in to see if I wanted any drugs prescribed, and decided to take her back to Theatre. Poor Angela had lost quite a lot of blood and lay very quiet for a week after. She recovered completely in time, and before she left the ward was threatening to tell Daddy about no end of things.

Sometimes detective work pays dividends in the nursing profession. Little Mark was admitted with a fractured jaw to be set under general anaesthetic. Talking to him while I was getting him ready, I learned that he had broken his jaw playing football. "I didn't 'alf get an 'ammering too nurse, I aint supposed to play running games 'cos of my bad 'eart." This chance remark set me rummaging furiously through his casualty notes. There was no mention of any heart disease. I was ready to put it down to a small boy's imagination when some intuition made me enquire further. I picked up the desk phone and rang the Cardiac department of the Children's hospital. Sure enough, young Mark's name was high on their list of serious cardiac lesions. Just as this was confirmed the trolley arrived to take him to Theatre. I had to go up and explain to an irate Houseman that he couldn't have my patient, and when I gave my reasons his attitude changed. I was commended for being observant. That incident put me in well with that Houseman for the remainder of my time at the hospital.

There is a block system of training in most teaching hospitals nowadays. This means part of the training is spent on the wards, gaining practical experience, and part of it is spent in the classroom receiving lectures from Surgeons, Physicians and Sisters. Sir Jacob Schwarz, a well known bacteriologist, always seasoned his lectures with little experiments and amazing statistics and so held us all spellbound. One miserable Monday afternoon when we were preparing to endure the last lecture of a long day. Sir Jacob strode briskly to the platform and announced that, as it was such a dull day and we wouldn't pay attention anyway, we could skip the lecture. Instead we could go down to the wards and take a swab of every place in the wards that might be a source of infection. We were to write a little chart with the time, place, and ward where the swab was taken, and return it to the laboratory for culture. Skinny Morris (she only weighed 6 stone) and I went dashing down to Male Surgical, sure that if any place in the hospital abounded with micro organisms it was there. Unfortunately, half the class had the same idea, and when we arrived, a harassed Sister Jamieson called from the office, "the only place they haven't invaded is the bathroom, you can try that if you like, but get Daddy Graham out first." We opened the bathroom door find old Mr Graham up to his neck in the bath, and by no means ready to come out. Skinny and I looked at each other, and by mutual unspoken consent, she dipped the swab in the bathwater and we both fled leaving Mr Graham with a bewildered expression on his face. The following week we waited as the results of the swabs were read out. Bacillus Coli were found in Male Surgical bathroom, we were informed.

Bacillus Coli is a normal inhabitant of the human colon or small intestine.

Chapter 5

Babies are notorious for arriving at inopportune times. Eleven o clock one evening I was just preparing to go home and sink into a warm comfortable bed when the phone rang. Could I put up an extra bed and find a cot from somewhere! A cot! Ours not being a maternity hospital the only cots were in storage behind stacks of old bed rests, drip bottles and other store room junk. Eventually, with the aid of two burly porters, a cot was procured. Our patient turned out to be a girl of 18 or so, one glance told me that the birth was imminent. Charming, I thought. I had never even seen a delivery. Anyway, I reflected, nature must take its course, which it did and I was just in time to deliver the head of a 4lb infant. Fortunately for the mother and for me, the Night Sister arrived on duty at that moment and efficiently took the situation out of my hands, while I slunk off to a late bed to dream of quads and things.

Another baby that arrived on the ward that same week - things usually go in runs - was Caroline, 1lb 9ozs. The mother was in for investigation of hyperemesis, excessive vomiting. She was an exceptionally highly strung girl, never still for a moment. She tended to make the most of her aches and pains, and when she complained of tummy ache Nurse Mann was rather callous. "Here's an aspirin, now go to sleep." Ten minutes later there was a yell from down the ward, "Oh! Come quick, nurse, the baby's coming." It was panic stations for a few minutes while an incubator was made ready and another cot unearthed from the glory hole. Sister, Houseman, nurses, students and ward maids arrived miraculously on the scene. Then began the great fight to save Caroline. She was like a very small chicken, she couldn't cry or make any noise and was a kind of bluish colour. For a month she stayed in a special side ward we had prepared and someone was detailed to keep a special watch on her day and night. There were weeks of painstaking nursing care, offset by one or two crises, once when she stopped breathing and again when she wouldn't eat, but very slowly her weight went up. She gained just a few ounces at a time, until in a month she was able to be transferred to a proper maternity hospital. Today Caroline is a buxom healthy school child.

Heather Ward, the, 'gynae,' ward was always hectic but everyone enjoyed working there. Sister Robson, a tiny slip of a woman, weighing just about six and a half stone, had a free and easy disposition, she took everything in her stride. It made no difference to her if she only had one nurse and three abortions were coming in, together with a few haemorrhages and a fibroids as well. She was often to be seen with her sleeves rolled up, elbow deep in the ward work, and the ward always ran like clockwork. Few people can really take emergencies in their stride and come out unruffled, but Robbie could.

Carol Dobson was admitted for investigations of abdominal pain and persistent high temperature. After a week of penicillin and bed rest she was still the same. It was decided that she should have a laparotomy to investigate the cause of the pain.

When the incision was made a piece of knitting needle was found embedded in the wall of her uterus and an abscess had formed around it. It was removed and stitched up and she was sent back to the ward to make a good recovery. This was one of the luckier attempts at abortion. Some of the less lucky ones didn't make it to the ward. They stopped in one of the outbuildings.

Mrs Mansford was admitted for investigations of infertility, They had been married for ten years, and although they both longed for a family she never conceived. All the routine tests were made and found to be normal. The Consultant told her that there was no reason on earth why she should not start a family. Mrs Manford burst into tears and said that they had desperately wanted children for years, and just couldn't have any. Sir Lennox then said an unusual thing. "Can you afford a holiday?" she could. "Then I advise you to go on a Mediterranean cruise and forget all about hospitals and families for a while. Just enjoy yourselves and come and see me within three months of coming back." When she came six months later, her face was radiant. Sir Lennox simply confirmed her pregnancy and sent her home with his congratulations. When a little boy arrived the Mansfords were delighted. Strangely enough, he had a little sister within two years. Afterwards, Sister asked Sir Lennox what was so special about a Mediterranean cruise. "I've no idea, but it often works," he beamed.

The term 'to special' a patient simply means keeping a 24 hour watch on him, recording temperature, pulse rate and respirations at 15 minute intervals. This is only done with gravely ill patients, and usually a nurse has to 'special' a patient only about 4 or 5 times a year. This was not so on Lyndon ward, the neuro surgery centre. There, every patient had to be specialled for at least 24 hours after an operation. There were about 8 nurses and about 6 patients to be specialled every other day. They were warded in little cubicles and the only effective way to run the ward was to arrange a rota of 6 special nurses and 2 runners. The duty of the runners was to relieve the special nurses for meals, answer the bells, attend to the other patients and generally handle any emergencies. Frequently the cubicle alarm bells would buzz and the runner would be back and forth all day. Mrs Brown was recovering from an operation to remove a cerebral tumour. It was her first day after the operation. The red light flashing from her cubicle summoned the runner, who arrived to see Mrs Brown foaming at the mouth and twitching and a horrible blue colour. Oxygen was administered, and gradually the seizure passed, but her breathing was hard and laboured and her pupils were unequal. No sooner had the runner left to attend to the ward when the alarm bell went again. Mrs Brown was having another fit. This went on all day and all night, with the runner worked off her feet. Morning came and Mrs Brown was barely conscious, with no outward signs of improvement. She stayed semi comatose for a week, then gradually began to notice things around her.

A fortnight after the operation she was allowed to get up and sit in a chair. When she got back to bed she promptly had another fit and repeated the process of the previous fortnight. Another week passed and she was allowed up again, this time she remained well and from then on made a good recovery. She was allowed home the next month and now she keeps a little shop with her husband.   Another patient we had cause to remember was Bill Morgan. He was admitted with serious head injuries after an accident down at the docks. An emergency craniotomy was performed and he was sent back to the ward. For the next few days he was deeply unconscious then gradually he began to recover. Within three weeks he was up and about helping with the ward in general. One morning Nurse Trelawney was doing his dressing when he picked up a glass from his locker threatened to hit her with it if she didn't leave him alone. She left him alone!   That night the night nurse found him prowling around the kitchen with a fork in his hand. She managed to get him back to bed and phoned for the Houseman to prescribe some heavy sleeping drugs. Bill seemed quiet the next day but he stayed in bed and ignored everybody. When his wife came to visit him he grew very agitated and threatened her. He developed a habit of glancing all around him and became more and more withdrawn. Specialists were called in and an encephalogram was taken. Unfortunately, scar tissue had begun to form in the site of Bill's fractured skull, causing marked personality changes. What had been a normal young man became a potentially dangerous criminal. He had to be kept under heavy sedation and was finally discharged to a psychiatric hospital.

Tetanus is a rare disease these days, and so it was unusual to have five cases of it on the ward all at once. Tetanus is characterised by spasms of all the muscles, especially the face and neck muscles, hence the name, 'lockjaw.' It is a disease which, above all else, demands devoted nursing care and absolute quiet. Even the slamming of a door can cause a patient to go into a series of fresh spasms. The respiratory muscles are affected, so it often used to be fatal. The modern treatment is to give the patient injections of curare, the poison that Auca Indians put on their poison darts. It is obtained from the chinchona bark. This completely paralyses the patient and he breathes by means of an artificial respirator. The patient can see and hear everything, but is unable to move a muscle. Of course, they are tranquilised to minimise the stress this causes. There is an endless nursing routine for such people. They have to be turned every half hour to prevent pressure sores, the respirator has to be checked every fifteen minutes and they are fed through a tube every hour. Their temperature, pulse and respirations are checked every half hour and if there is any sign of muscle spasm anywhere, more curare is given. This treatment ensures complete rest for as long as the germ is active in the body, then gradually the dose of the drug is reduced and the patient is weaned off the respirator.

Mrs Harding weighed eighteen stone, she contracted tetanus when she stepped on a rake in her garden. Turning an eighteen stone woman every half hour is no easy task, especially when she cannot move at all. Often if a person is unable to move, one tends to think she cannot see and hear either. Weeks later, when Mrs Harding was up and about, she would remind us of the rude remarks we nurses made about her elephantine proportions when we had forgotten that she could hear us.

Luckily, she was so grateful to be alive that she took it in good part.

Bathtime is often the highlight of the nurses day. Not because she can sink into a warm bath, but because she can spend a comfortable ten minutes or so on the bathroom stool while one of her patients has a bath. It is quite a companionable time for the nurse. Sometimes patients will wax voluble when they are in the bath. It is quite pleasant to relax on the bathroom stool and hear all about Mrs Lawson's divorce, or how Mrs Reed's husband is carrying on. Old Mr Parry detested his bath. He was pushing 90 years of age and could count the number of baths he had had on his one hand. Every morning there was the same scene as we tried to persuade him to have a bath. "'Taint necessary, all this washing," he would say, or, "I 'ad a bath only yesterday." That was when he was in a reasonable mood, if he wasn't he would curse and swear all up and down the ward. On those days we gave in and he stayed dirty.

Thursdays were always a big day on Phillips Ward. It was the Cardiac Ward and served people from a vast area. Many children were admitted to correct cardiac defects. Hole in the heart operations were quite common as the hospital drew patients from practically everywhere. There would be two teams of Theatre staff, and they would work non stop from 8am to 4pm on one patient. The one team would relieve the other for a quick sandwich snack in the ante room then they would be back again, changing into new sterile masks and gowns to continue the delicate task of tying off the arteries and repairing atrophied tissue. Another team of specialists would be attending to the apparatus for hypothermia. Open heart surgery is carried out while the body is chilled to about 33degrees C, and the patient is kept alive by the heart and lung machine. Young Carol Harvey was a teenager admitted to Phillips Ward for investigation of acute breathlessness and cyanosis. When she came in it was all she could do to walk to the bed, and once in bed she lacked the vitality to even speak. There was an ugly greyish blue tinge to her skin and she could not speak more than a few words without getting breathless. The investigations took some weeks, and as Carol got to know all the different nurses on the ward, they would chat by her bed when Sister was away at meals or off duty. We got to know her very well. The day fixed for her operation was an anxious day for us all. Naturally, there is a certain element of risk with open heart surgery, and we had come to regard Carol as a friend. The Theatre porter came to the ward, and he would give us 'bulletins' as he called them. At 6pm, the phone rang, "would we come and collect our patient." Carol was barely conscious when she was wheeled into the ward, she was put straight into an oxygen tent and nurse Williams was detailed to 'special' her. All that night the nurses worked non stop with blood transfusions, changing oxygen cylinders, taking temperature pulse and respirations every 15 minutes and checking the incision. When morning came Carol was able to smile at us and complain about the drip in her arm. "Huh, you're getting better," snorted nurse Williams. She was right, Carol had a normal pinkish colour in her cheeks and, although she was very tired there was no sign of breathlessness. She left the ward some weeks later, completely well and has been leading a normal life ever since. The surgeons had repaired a hole in her heart the size of a modern 1 penny piece.

People talk of the miracle of surgery, but to the surgeon, this more a question of hard and conscientious study of methods, new sterile techniques to try out, experimenting with existing methods and devising new ones. Drama is so much part of a hospital life that the hospital staff tend to grow hardened. It has often been said that nothing should surprise a nurse, and indeed, after seeing a cross section of a normal general hospital, nothing will surprise her. There is one case, however, that springs to mind whenever people gather and the conversation turns to nursing and the exciting lives we must lead. It started off like any other day on the ward, no one was particularly ill and the routine ward work was well under way. Sister was off duty for the morning, and I was availing myself of the opportunity to snatch a quick cup of coffee in her office and browse through her magazines. A buzzing noise somewhere above my head indicated that one of the patients needed attention. 'Another bed pan', I thought vindictively, 'well, he can wait', and, as there were other nurses on the ward I settled myself down to finish my coffee. Bzz, Bzz, it went again, still I ignored it, Then again, more urgently this time. Exasperated, I stalked into the ward and found two or three of the ambulant patients around Mr Jordan's bed. His face was greyish blue and contorted and his breathing was laboured. Grabbing the oxygen apparatus in one hand and pressing the emergency call button with the other, I rushed to the bed. At a glance I could tell he had had a seizure of some kind. In the short time it took to assemble the oxygen mask, Mr Jordan had stopped breathing and no pulse was perceptible. With the help of one of the other patients I positioned him and started mouth to mouth resuscitation and meanwhile the Houseman and Registrar appeared. Bob Flaherty, the Houseman took over from me while I grabbed the resuscitation tray which contained the defibrillator. There was a very faint pulse at the wrist after about three minutes. The Registrar then started closed cardiac massage, a method of massaging the heart without incision to the chest. After some minutes of this there was no even heart rhythm, and the pulse was imperceptible. He picked up a scalpel from the tray, "Give us a number 5 blade, nurse." He made a swift incision into the thoracic cavity, retracted the third and fourth rib, and began rhythmically and evenly to squeeze the heart against the sternum. Almost immediately Mr Jordan's face lost its extreme pallor and the pulse was again felt at the wrist. The theatre trolley arrived and he was whisked away to be stitched up and for the registrar to see the extent of damage to the heart muscle. It must be stressed that in cases of cardiac arrest where the heart just stops everything possible must be done to revive the patient. It is far better to open the chest wall and massage the heart without anaesthetic (the patient being unconscious) than to use hit or miss methods until you can get him to Theatre by which time it is probably too late. Mr Jordan's case was to prove interesting, because the same thing happened on three subsequent occasions it the next fortnight. He is reasonably fit and well today and attends out patients clinic every six months for a check up.

Dai Davies was one of the long term patients on Harper Ward, a tough weatherbeaten Welshman, he had been tramping the country for about twenty years getting work where he could find it, but not if he could avoid it. He was brought in more dead than alive one evening, having collapsed in a pub down by the docks. The young Houseman who took the case, thinking probably of the circumstances of Dai's admission to hospital, diagnosed excess of alcohol as the cause for his collapse. As far as we were concerned he was just another patient. Nobody took much notice of his condition, and so we were all rather surprised when Night Sister summoned us all into her office, "Now," she said crisply. "About Mr Davies." And she produced his charts. "What's his pulse rate, Nurse Jenkins?" "110, sister," I stammered, "His temperature, Nurse Owen," "96, sister," "what's the condition of his skin, Nurse Jeffreys?" "I - I don't know Sister," she stammered, "Go and find out." She came back. "Cold and sweating," she reported. " Right, now, these signs and symptoms. Are they consistent with just being drunk?" There was silence. "Cold, clammy skin, low body temperature, high, weak pulse, what's the picture?" she demanded. "Haemorrhage or shock," ventured Nurse Jeffreys timidly, "Exactly," said Sister reaching for the phone. "Now go, prepare a blood transfusion trolley, a theatre pack and a complete examination tray." As we slunk out we heard Sister's ominous tones. "Get me Lyons." (the young Houseman). Unfortunately we didn't hear the end of that conversation, but it would probably have proved interesting. Old Dai was found to have a bleeding gastric ulcer. It had been slowly bleeding for some time and he was in a poor condition. An immediate blood transfusion was ordered, and a course of drugs to prevent haemorrhage. Probably because Sister had brought his case to our attention, we were all particularly interested in old Dai. We watched his progress from day to day. The immediate need was to get him into a better physical state and thus minimise the dangers of operation. Some three weeks later it was decided that they would do a partial gastrectomy. Two days before the set date he went down with pleurisy. A month later, having nursed him back into a reasonable physical condition, a date was fixed again. This time he fell out of bed and dislocated his shoulder. Postponed again. A week after that he was made ready for operation again. This time he was prepared, and even put on the theatre trolley. On the way to theatre the escort nurse noticed that he was a peculiar colour. When they got to theatre his breathing was harsh and gasping. It was discovered that he had had a pulmonary embolism - a small clot of blood blocking one of the vessels in his lungs. Dai was taken back to the ward, seriously ill. It was touch and go for the next few days and a long convalescence after that. During this time we got to know him well, and he got to know how the ward was run. He would sometimes help us with teas, and if a new nurse wanted to know anything she would creep up and ask old Dai rather than risk a, "you should know that by now," from one of us. He possessed a fine baritone voice and most mornings from the bathroom drifted the strains of 'men of Harlech,' or, 'Flow gently sweet Afton,' if he was in a more mellow mood. All the suffering he had been through, and the number of times he had been face to face with death did nothing to dim his inbred cheerfulness. Sometimes, of an evening we would gather round his bed when the ward work was done and he would keep us spellbound with stories of his travels. He would paint vivid word pictures of his days in the Welsh coal mines. How, as a boy of 14 he would lead the pit ponies along the labyrinth of roads underground. "Blind as bats they was, mun, never seen daylight, see." Stories of explosions underground, of how a fire raged for years in Senghenydd colliery. We would hold our breath as he told of the dreaded, 'after damp.' The colourless, odourless gas that would collect down the mine after an explosion, and how the miners would be found. "Dead as mutton, see, with cheeks as red as a day in Barry Island." He told how rescuers used to take canaries in cages down the mine. "One whiff of gas and over they'd go, stone dead," he'd say. At last it was decided for the fourth time to operate. This time all went smoothly, the operation was completed and Dai was brought back to the ward. He made a good recovery for some weeks, then one morning in the middle of the breakfast rush, he just collapsed and died within a matter of minutes. Post mortem examination revealed a massive pulmonary embolism. Hospital wards are so used to life and death that there is little emotion felt usually, but Parker Ward was overcast that day. Old Dai had said many times that he would leave the ward feet first, but no one took any notice. Could he have known, somehow, we wondered.

Coming down to breakfast at some unearthly hour on a bitterly cold morning I came across a crowd gathered round the notice board, my heart sank. Six weeks is the usual time to spend on any one ward and I had already spent two months on Parker. I had grown accustomed to the ward routine and formed a firm friendship with the staff, and even Sister was bearable. Now to be dragged away and plunged into yet another alien ward. This was the last straw. Fighting my way forward for a better view of the board I read - Nurse Jenkins, Smith Ward. Yet again my heart sank. Smith Ward was a student nurses nightmare, a sort of ward that one hopes Sister Admin will forget about when compiling the nurses schedule. She never does. The

Sister on Smith ward was one of the old school. Fortunately, her kind are rapidly becoming extinct. On Smith Ward student nurses were classed in three grades, rather stupid, rather more stupid, and congenital idiots. Sister Overton was middle aged, a sergeant major type with a voice to match. Hence my apprehension. Otorhinolaryngology - ear nose and throat, to the uninitiated, - covers a varied and interesting field. It can range from tiny babies with cleft palates to extremely old men with tumours of the vocal cords. In the hectic six weeks on Smith Ward I encountered the lot. I had always dreaded being put on an E.N.T. Ward. No one minds a straight forward gastric ulcer or appendix except, of course, the patient, but there is something disconcerting about a patient who can only converse by putting his finger over a hole in his throat and hissing at you. Mrs Weaver was admitted for investigations of recurrent laryngitis. A tracheotomy was performed, this is an opening into the trachea in the midline of the throat. A metal, or more currently, a plastic tube is inserted into this opening, and through this, the patient breathes. As Sister

Overton pointed out, at great length, there are dangers, and special nursing care is required for these patients. This tiny hole, about half an inch round is all they have to breathe through. If this should become blocked either by mucus when they cough, or by a blanket, the consequences could be serious. Mary Owen and I were doing the evening drinks round, congratulating ourselves that we had got through a day untouched by Sister's scathing tongue. Maybe we were lulled into a sense of false security by the fact that she had gone off duty, (an hour or so late, as usual) We took very little notice when there was a prolonged whoop from somewhere up the ward. The noise was repeated yet again. There are many strange noises on any hospital ward, especially on ear nose and throat ward. The trained ear knows instinctively the dangerous noises. As yet, our ears were untrained. Coming to Mrs Weavers bed we found her blue and choking, clutching frantically at the blankets. Acting on orders implanted forever in our minds by the stentorian tones of Sister Overton, Nurse Owen grabbed the suction apparatus (the sucker). And I grabbed Mrs Weaver. Obviously something had lodged in her tracheotomy tube. The action of sitting her up must have dislodged the object because she stopped choking and whooping almost at once. We could find nothing in the tracheotomy tube though, so there was something still in her trachea. Any foreign body is a potential source of danger, so we decided to contact the duty surgeon. He arrived promptly, stethoscope dangling from starched white coat, beneath which protruded yellow pyjama clad legs. He poked and prodded at poor Mrs Weavers throat but could not find anything so he decided to do a bronchoscopy. Theatre was contacted and Mrs Weaver was prepared, with much complaining. "Don't know what 'ee be bothering about, I b'aint choking now," half an hour later she was wheeled back to the ward, peacefully asleep. The porter handed Mary a swab, "with the compliments of the Houseman." She opened it up and discovered a sultana, the foreign body. Mrs Weaver had obviously had cake for tea.

Working on Casualty is an experience in itself although the nurse doesn't establish much contact with the patients. They come and are transferred to the wards quickly, so they are seldom remembered for long by casualty staff. Certain characters are seldom forgotten, though. One such person was Rita Patel. She was admitted via casualty one evening, the victim of a road accident. She had dislocated her shoulder and had severe head injuries, she was deeply unconscious. Rita was Indian by birth, true to tradition, she wore a beautiful silk sari fastened at the shoulder by a large jade brooch. The duty of the Casualty nurse is to admit all new patients, take their particulars and get them in to bed in hospital linen ready for examination by the Doctor. This evening had been busier than usual and the three nurses on duty were rushing around with no time even for a coffee break. Nurse Owen admitted Rita, and as she was unconscious, put the admission forms aside until the morning and started to undress her. This was where the trouble started, try as she might, Mary Owen couldn't fathom out how the sari came off. She called Nurse Knight, who in turn called me. We must have been puzzling it out for some time because the work in Casualty was piling up and patients were beginning to complain. Eventually, Sister poked her head around the screen to see what was causing the delay. She summed up the situation quickly, and after trying to remove Rita's sari herself, she rang Lucas Smith Ward. "Send Nurse Demades down here, will you." she asked, and went on to explain the problem. Carla Demades was a Pakistani nurse, and obviously she would know how to remove a sari from an unconscious patient. Carla came and unwound yards and yards of sari from Rita. If we had tried for hours we couldn't have fathomed out how it came off. When Rita was sitting up in bed a few days later she was amused to hear all about it She gave us all a demonstration of how to put on a sari, using Carla as a model.

Another unusual character who arrived via Casualty was Tony Smith, a young man of about 34. He came limping in one evening with a nail in his foot. This was removed, the wound dressed and he was sent home. A few weeks later he came limping in again with a piece of glass in the same foot. Again it was dressed and he was sent home, probably with an admonition about walking around without his shoes. Some days after that, Tony came in again. This time he had a septic wound in his foot. His pulse rate and temperature were up and he had signs of septicaemia. This time he was admitted and went to Theatre to have the foot sorted out. Deep down in the wound there was a piece of a needle broken off. The Houseman and Sister had a consultation about this. It happened too often to be left to coincidence. They decided to tackle Tony and find out what was going on. He was sullen and uncommunicative and would not say anything in answer to their queries. It was the nurses who found out the reason, some weeks later. It appeared that Tony had been engaged and his fiancée had broken it off. He had been deliberately treading on nails and things in the hope that he would be admitted to hospital. He thought that if his ex-fiancée saw him in hospital she might feel sorry that she had broken off the engagement. Sad to say, Tony ended up in the Psychiatric ward and his ex-fiancée didn't even visit him.

Mary and John Doolan were a honeymoon couple who had been involved in a motor cycle accident. John had fractured both legs and a collar bone. Mary had bruised ribs and concussion. They were admitted to the Orthopaedic Wards. The male and female orthopaedic wards were at either end of a long corridor, and the domestic staff and nurses were continually requested to carry notes between Mary and John. They came in for a lot of good natured teasing from the Ward staff, especially as Mary was so stunned on admission that she had given her maiden name to the nurse on duty. Mary was up and about first and she used to spend part of the day at John's bedside. Whenever mealtimes came around and she was nowhere to be found, one of us would pick up the phone and say, "tell Mary to come for her dinner."

Christmas in a hospital is an exciting time. All rules are relaxed and practically anything goes. For weeks before the day there are no end of preparations going on, rehearsals for student pantomimes, decorations being made, and last year's decorations being dug out and renovated.

Each ward usually takes a theme for Christmas, one ward may represent Treasure Island, another, Robinson Crusoe or the City of London. The nurses make fantastic tableaux of all sorts of thing to illustrate their particular theme. The excitement grows and grows as they get more and more busy. The patients do all they can in the way of painting and giving suggestions. On Christmas day the night nurses come round just before going off duty singing carols, holding candles, and wearing their cloaks. The Surgeon carves the turkey at dinner time and everyone has dinner on the ward. There is a great deal of coming and going in all the wards, and very little work done. One Christmas morning the day nurses, arriving on duty, were confronted by the sight of screens and a blood transfusion stand at the first bed by the door. The night staff gave them a quick report on the patients. The patient by the door had been admitted during the night and was dangerously ill. They were not holding out any hope for her. Somewhat dismayed by this turn of events on Christmas day, we went behind the screens to attend to the new patient. We saw a shrivelled figure huddled under the bedclothes, just a dishevelled mop of hair was visible. We went closer to see the patient, when the bedclothes shot back and out jumped Bridget Callaghan, one of the junior nurses. "Thought you were in for a bit of work, didn't you," she laughed. By the time she came on duty that evening we had planted explosive cigarettes in the box on the desk and filled a sherry bottle with vinegar by way of revenge.

Chapter 6

Early in the first year of training the nurse learns to give injections. Most nurses will admit that whatever procedures they may carry out later, the first injection is always a daunting experience. I had been on Rutherford Ward for about two weeks when Staff Nurse Jones approached with a business like expression. She was holding a covered dish. "Ah, Nurse Jenkins," she beamed. "In this receiver I have two mega units of penicillin, you are going to watch me give one and you, yourself, are going to give the next one." Before I could open my mouth we were at Mrs Harrison's bedside. She was a plump cheerful soul of about 45 or 50 years. Expertly Staff Nurse Jones gave the penicillin. "Lovely, dear, I didn't feel a thing." Mrs Harrison smiled. Then again before I could say a word we were at the next bed. Mrs Amies was a complete contrast. She was thin and angular with a gaunt face and a complaining manner. I must have appeared uneasy, as Mrs Amies grunted, "Hmmph, practising on me again, nurse eh! Well, mind you do it properly or Sister will hear about it." This was enough to unnerve anyone no matter how long they had been giving injections. Trying to stop my hand from shaking, I raised the syringe. Shutting my eyes, I held my breath and jabbed. I felt the needle go in, and no doubt Mrs Amies did as well. I injected the penicillin and withdrew the syringe. Breathing a sigh of relief, we walked back up the ward. When we were out of earshot Staff Nurse Jones said, "Not bad, but there were two things you did wrong, - first of all, when you inject a patient you always withdraw the needle a fraction to see if you've hit a blood vessel. Secondly, when you withdraw the needle you always keep your hand on the surrounding skin so that the it comes out easily." In time I perfected the technique of giving injections, but that first one I always remember.

There is a lot of controversy in the medical profession as to the correct method of giving an injection. Some say that if the nurse slaps the skin then quickly gives the injection, the patient is so surprised by the slap that he doesn't feel the needle going in. This has been known to work. Others say that the syringe should be held like a dart, the skin stretched, and the needle introduced quickly. This is the method I found best. Then again the nurse may pinch the skin and slide the needle in with her forefinger on the needle. This I found both painful and unhygienic, strictly for amateurs. The most unusual method I came across in my training was employed by a continental nurse. She would balance the syringe on the back of her hand and, with a flick of her wrist the syringe would fly into the air, somersault once, and always land on the exact spot of the patient's anatomy that she wanted it to. Though I tried time and time again, not, of course on the patients, I could never get this method to work. Evidently it must have taken years of practise.

The two most difficult types of patient as far as injections are concerned, are very fat patients and athletic young men. The former are difficult because the needle goes up to the hilt in the fat of the patients thigh and not into the muscle. The latter, because the thigh muscles are so well developed and strong that the needle will not penetrate. My colleagues and I have bent many a needle on this type of patient. There has always been some controversy as to the actual site of an intramuscular injection. Whether to give it into the thigh and risk the patient having a stiff leg for a few hours, or into the buttock and run the risk of hitting the sciatic nerve. Nurse Wilson had a frightening experience while we were on casualty together. A young dockhand had been admitted with extensive lacerations and bruising after, "a night out with the boys," as he said. The Houseman ordered a mega unit of penicillin to combat possible infection. Nurse Wilson gave the injection into his buttock and immediately he complained of pins and needles down his leg. She came dashing into the sluice to tell me and to find out if anything could be done. "Don't say anything," said Mary Wilson, and see if it wears off." We both decided to wait a quarter of an hour and see if the pins and needles would go, and if they didn't, Mary would have to go and confess her crime. After about five minutes we had a look at the boy, he was still ruefully rubbing his leg. At the end of fifteen minutes we went anxiously to look again. This time he gave the thumbs up sign, the pins and needles had gone. We both breathed a tremendous sigh of relief. Mary had evidently nicked the end of the sciatic nerve or passed close enough to disturb it. After that she never gave an intramuscular injection anywhere but in the thigh muscle, and neither did I. A good tip that we were taught in Preliminary Training School was to always give intramuscular injections in the upper, outer quadrant of the patient's buttock, thereby missing the sciatic nerve. The nurse would trace an imaginary cross on the patient's buttock and place the needle in the top left quarter, or the top right, depending on which side she was injecting.

It was a major catastrophe in my training hospital if a patient fell out of bed. There would be report sheets to be filled in, a signed statement to go to Matron's office and probably an interview as well. Patients were not allowed out of bed between the hours of 10pm and 6am, and if Night Sister found anyone out of bed when she did her rounds, there would be trouble for the nurse in charge of the ward. Mrs Denning was an old lady with chronic cystitis, a long lasting inflammation of the bladder. Consequently, every hour of the day or night she would need to relieve herself. Being a kindly old soul she didn't like to trouble the nurse for a bedpan in the middle of the night so she would invariably try and creep out of bed to go to the toilet. No matter how many times the nurse would explain to her that this simply wasn't allowed, out she'd get and the nurse would sit holding her breath in case Night Sister came along and caught her. One night, when Mrs Denning had been out of bed about eight times, the night nurse could stand no more. She was very firm, and told her that this was positively the last time she would let her get out, and in future she would have to make do with a bedpan like everybody else. Evidently this unnerved poor old Mrs Denning, who, being old and feeble anyway, was none too steady on her feet. Halfway out of bed her foot slipped and although she didn't actually fall she caught a glancing blow to her elbow. Just as she was settled back into bed Night Sister came round. Seeing Mrs Denning still awake she stopped to ask if she needed anything. "I'm alright, sister," she replied, "but I didn't half bang my elbow just now." Of course, Night Sister wanted to know all about it, and she looked doubtful when the night nurse said that the old lady hadn't actually fallen.

When I think of night duty, the name Mrs Noble always springs to mind. She was a long term patient on Miller Ward. Any time of the day or night she could drink a cup of tea. I would come on duty at night, settle the patients down, give drinks out and sleeping tablets where they were needed. Mrs Noble would always be asleep when I came around with the drinks and drugs, and so miss them. It could be guaranteed that when Sister did her round about two hours later Mrs Noble would demand a sleeping tablet. "They missed me, see Sister." Then, when that was given she would say, "They missed me with the drinks, too, do you think I could have a cup of tea?" Sister soon got used to this, and when we explained to her that Mrs Noble was always asleep when we came on duty, she advised us to humour her and not wake her. She would only complain about being wakened up just when she had gone off to sleep. "Some patients enjoy a little moan, nurse," she would say. "Who are we to deprive them of it." The clanking of cups in the kitchen would wake up most of the other patients and it would finish up as a general tea round, with the resultant bedpan round all because of Mrs Noble. We had six night sisters in quick succession at one time. No sooner had the nurse got used to the idiosyncrasies of one when another would come to take her place. One in particular I remember. Sister Baines, whose one passion in life was to ensure that her patients got sufficient sleep. If a sleeping drug did not work one night, she would have a new one written up by the following night. She would come on the ward to do her round with a large torch, and as she went from bed to bed she would direct this beam of light at each patients face to see if they were asleep. "Oh aye," snorted the porter one night, "There goes Baines, waking them up to see if they're asleep."

The one that succeeded her was Sister Martin. We all liked her, probably because she had not yet acquired the rather starchy air that most other sisters have. It was her first Sisters post and, as yet she lacked confidence. I'm afraid we rather tended to take advantage of that fact. In general training the nurse touches on most fields of nursing and later she may take special courses in any particular branch that she fancies. Many trained nurses who have no desire to stay at their training hospital as Staff Nurses, and do not want to go on to do midwifery, may take up to seven or eight special courses in different hospitals before their wanderlust is satisfied. They usually end up married or as Sisters at their training hospital, as to every nurse, her own training hospital is always the best. Sister Martin had taken courses in Infectious diseases, Oncology, Neurosurgery and Chest surgery before finally settling down to be a junior Night Sister. The knowledge she had acquired was brought to play one busy night in Casualty. In the space of two hours we had admitted a little boy with an unidentified rash and a high temperature who was barely conscious, a road accident victim with a fractured skull and spine, an old lady with an internal haemorrhage and a young man with a collapsed lung. Now there are specialised procedures for nursing each of these patients and we, as junior nurses, were hastily thumbing through our textbooks to refresh our memories. Sister Martin took in the situation at a glance. "Right," she said. "Nurse Evans, you take the little boy, Nurse Mead, the haemorrhage, Nurse Jenkins, the road accident, and I'll take the collapsed lung." Then she went to each cubicle giving precise instructions as to the treatment of each patient. All she needed to know was there at her fingertips and her experience of different cases gave her confidence to handle a situation where many would have been overwhelmed. The little boy was found to have encephalitis, a rare complication of chicken pox. The old lady had a malignant growth that had slowly eroded through an artery wall. Most of them, suitably patched up, left hospital in a few weeks.

Nurses are notorious for referring to patients, not by their names but by their ailments. For example, "the prolapse in bed 4," or, "the adenoids in bed 5." At one time, Matron was quite concerned about this and started a campaign to try and get everyone to refer to patients by their names. Tradition dies hard though, and for generations nurses all over the world have been doing the same thing, calling patients by their diseases, so we continued to do so. Another expression that Matron tried to change was, 'the office said.' The staff in Matron's office, that is, everyone from Matron down to the clerk are known as, 'the office.' Whatever the new rule was, if it came from the office, it was, "The office said caps must have no pleats or tucks," or, "the office said we may not have more than two inches taken off the length of our uniform dresses." There were many of these little rules to make nurses uniforms less attractive. The uniform shoes were a constant source of irritation. They were the most ungainly part of the whole uniform. Flat, clumsy round toed laceups. Several petitions went to the office to be allowed to wear something smarter, preferably by Clarks, but they were repeatedly and pointedly ignored. In the end most nurses just wore Clarks and said nothing, but kept uniform shoes for examinations and prize days.

Ultra violet light is used in most hospitals these days for the treatment of acne and various skin diseases. There was an ultra violet lamp on Mennon Ward. It was the subject of much discussion when the night nurses met in the sitting room. Carol Barker was heard to remark that she wouldn't mind a Riviera tan to go on holiday with. We were all rather amused when, on the next change list Carol's name was down to go on Mennon ward. The next night she informed us that she was going to sit under the lamp and get tanned slowly. For the first two or three nights she sat under for four minutes, gradually increasing to seven minutes, but there was no change at all in her skin. She then decided to get a tan all at once and sat for half an hour. When she came for coffee at midnight her cheeks were quite pink and we all thought it was going to work, but when she came for breakfast her face was so puffed up and red that her eyes were just slits. Of course, she couldn't go to sick quarters because they would know what she had done, so all that day she lay in bed with a bottle of calamine lotion and a pad of cotton wool. By the evening it was a little better and she went on duty. Three or four days later her face started to peel and she looked like nothing on earth. Nothing was said by the Ward Sister, but after that the sun lamp was locked up.

The subject of money in the medical profession has long been a controversial one. Some say that medical work is a labour of love, and that doctors and nurses ought to be prepared to work long hours for next to nothing. Others say that they should be more highly paid than most professions. Most student nurses take the latter view. There have been disputes about nurses pay as long as the nursing profession has been established. There was a nationwide dispute about it some years back. Apparently, the nurses wanted more than the government said they could afford. It was the main talking point whenever we met together in the common room. Letters were written by irate student nurses to the papers, parliament, one even to the

Queen herself. Protest marches were arranged and general interest was aroused. Young Carol Mannering wrote to the Minister of Health, signing herself 'disgusted'. We were all expecting a reply addressed to, 'Dear disgusted,' but none came. Even the dockworkers had a day's strike and went on a protest march for us. We got our pay rise. Not a lot, but it was something. For months after that, every time anyone had a grievance, which was often, we would speculate about having another march. The salary a junior nurse received before qualifying was definitely not enough to live on. It was not uncommon for student nurses to take part time jobs to supplement their pay. This, of course was strictly against all the rules and regulations of most hospitals. During my third year of training I found that saving to get married was impossible. I had to live as well. I took a job as a part time waitress in a coffee bar. This went quite well for two or three months, although I always dreaded that one of the staff would come in as a customer. That would have been my nursing career finished. One evening a young man came in, his face looked vaguely familiar but I was too busy to notice much. The next morning I was listening to Sister reading the night report when the Houseman strolled in. Our eyes met. It was with a feeling of shock I recognised the man from the previous day. He opened his mouth to say something but instinctively, I put my finger to my lips. When Sister had finished and I was back in the ward he came across. "Hey, it wasn't you I saw in the Blue Anchor yesterday, was it?" he enquired. "Oh for heavens sake don't say anything," I pleaded. He was a sport and kept quiet, but I gave up the job anyway. It was getting near to State Finals and late nights coupled with early mornings were not conducive to study.

It was getting near to Finals when Sister Tutor discovered to her dismay that our set had not been to the plaster room. The plaster room is where all the techniques of Plaster of Paris is learned. Everything from a spinal plaster to a broken toe is taught in the plaster room. We all donned gigantic rubber aprons, collected rolls and rolls of Plaster of Paris bandage and went wild for the whole morning. We were in pairs and we practised different plaster techniques on each other. Grace Owen was my partner, she had had orthopaedic experience before and did a beautiful plaster on my ankle. I decided to do one on her arm. Following meticulously the instructions in my, 'practical nursing,' book, I bound her hand and arm with wet, sticky plaster and left it to harden. After a while she came up, an anxious expression on her face, "Hey, Maud, look at my fingers." I looked. They were blue and swollen, "I've got pins and needles," she whispered, "what shall we do?" "Cut it off of course," I said with much more bravado than I felt, and went in search of the plaster cutters. Has anyone ever seen a pair of plaster cutters? They are large vicious looking things and extremely difficult to manipulate. "Alright, put your arm on here," I said, pointing to the table. Trying to keep my own hands from trembling, I hooked one end of the cutters under the plaster, against her arm and squeezed. Nothing happened, the plaster didn't move. "You're not holding it right," she yelled as I tried again. This time it gave about an inch and the plaster started to part. "Go carefully," Grace pleaded, her voice trembling now. "Don't you think you had better fetch Sister?" "What, and get put on the carpet." I shouted indignantly. Finals were looming up and I couldn't afford a black mark. Eventually the plaster came off, and with it, a few pieces of Grace's arm. "Why the heck didn't you tell me it was cutting you," I asked. She replied that her arm was numb anyway and that she couldn't feel anything.

One often hears wild rumours about prowlers in the nurses home, and usually nobody takes any notice but there had been a series of murders and robberies with violence around the district where the hospital was located. In six weeks two girls had been found murdered and another three had narrowly escaped when they had been accosted. The nurses home was in a state of panic, we had all begun to demand double rooms and those who had rooms on the first floor or with windows near drainpipes marched to the Home Sister and demanded to be moved. One night, at the height of the trouble, Nurse Mannering woke up to hear footsteps outside her door. "They weren't girls footsteps," she said. We were all awakened by a ringing scream echoing and re-echoing down the corridors. The more timid of our crowd locked their doors and stayed where they were, while the adventurous ones went to investigate. Ganging up and arming ourselves with anything that came to hand, we advanced slowly in the direction of the scream. We found Carol Mannering in a sobbing heap on the floor of her room. She had heard footsteps, looked out and seen a man disappearing round the staircase. Immediately we all rushed down to the Home Sister's office. "Quick, there's a man in the home," I panted. "My dear girl," she replied calmly, "there are three men in the home, all plain clothes policemen and all here for your protection, now kindly go to sleep".

Most nurses had at some time or another, used the drainpipe and window method of entry into the nurses home, and knowing that it was possible to get in that way did nothing to enhance our feeling of impregnability. Sister Dunhill on Outpatients Department was a notorious busybody. She lived in the Sister's hostel overlooking the drive that led to the nurses home. This was known as, 'the virgin's retreat,' by the medical students. Few people came up and down the drive unobserved by Sister Dunhill if she was off duty. Nurse Parry had a boyfriend who was something of a beatnik. He wore dirty sweaters and jeans and sported a Van Dyck beard. Unlike the average beatnik, however, he owned a long smooth red sports car. It would come purring up the drive and stop with a flourish just below Sister Dunhill's window. This went on every night for a month, and eventually Sister's curiosity got the better of her. Cornering Jane Parry in the hospital corridor one day she remarked "I noticed your red car again last night, nurse." "Oh," replied Jane, slightly abashed, then decided to avoid an inquisition by telling all, she blurted out, "He's doing a three months course in structural design at the university, he's my fiancé and he comes from Leeds." In the face of this outburst even Sister Dunhill couldn't ask any more. With a brief. "Don't let anything interfere with your studies, nurse," she scuttled off. Many older nursing sisters are motivated by an intense curiosity, nosiness, as the students prefer to call it. Maybe the nursing profession attracts that type of person, or maybe living so close to eternal issues, in such close proximity to birth and death, they develop a yearning to share in the more ordinary pursuits.

I remember an eminent psychologist once saying to us in a lecture. "Life is a pattern, there are deep places and high places, one cannot live intensely all the time nor live on a tranquil plane for too long, otherwise psychiatric traits may begin to appear. One side of life complements the other."

Wherever catering is done on a large scale the food has a sameness to it. The potatoes taste the same as the porridge and the porridge tastes the same as the rice pudding. This is true with student's dining rooms, Army, Navy and Air Force messes, hostel cookhouses and almost everywhere else. A standard remark to be heard was, "chip flavoured doughnuts again." At one stage the food was really bad at our hospital. One night in the staff room (all plots are hatched and foul deeds conceived on night duty in the staff room) we decided to send a petition to Matron's office. This was duly drafted and signed by all except the goody goodies. The following day a notice went up on the board to say that all complaints regarding dining room administration were to be sent via the catering officer. A petition was sent to the catering officer. She ignored it. Another one was sent, she ignored that, too. Finally, three of the bravest of us asked for an interview. It was rather a stormy scene, with the catering officer, a temperamental girl of French origin wringing her hands and exclaiming that she was doing her best with a limited staff, and we three declaring that her best wasn't good enough. We thought the matter would be dropped, as ninetyfive percent of nurses complaint are, but a few days later we were surprised to see a procession three deep enter the dining room, with Matron in the lead. It was a surprise visit, we could tell that from the alarmed expressions on the faces of the voluble Italian kitchen maids. Nothing was said, but within a month we had a new catering officer and things improved a little although the porridge still tasted like blancmange. Encouraged and made bold by this turn of events, we were quick to organise another deputation when the cups began to get chipped and were not replaced. We marched to the catering officer first and then to Matron when the former took no notice. Matron gave us permission to smash every cracked cup we found in the dining room. This, she said was the only way to ensure that they were not used again. The news spread like wildfire through the ranks of students. We all went wild. If there is any truth in the rumour that breaking something relieves pent up emotions and inhibitions, there were many emotions liberated in the following days. The standard greeting for weeks after was. "Smashed any good crocs lately?"

Examinations have tendency to loom up from nowhere. One week they are somewhere in the distant future, and the next they are right on the doorstep. For several days before the Final hospital exams I had been confined to sick quarters with all the signs and symptoms of appendicitis, although the staff doctor would insist it was mesenteric adenitis. All nurses know best concerning their own ailments. It was touch and go whether I would be able to take the exams. I lay in sick quarters fretting and fuming with annoyance and frustration. It is a rule in sick quarters that no text books are allowed, and so I couldn't even swot anything up. The only thing I could quote with any assurance was the signs and symptoms of acute appendicitis. Two days before the exams I prevailed on the Houseman to let me out. I painted a tragic word picture of how my career would fall in ruins if I was imprisoned in sick quarters while the rest of our set took the exams. He gave in under my repeated reproaches and veiled threats - I happened to know the nurses he had been keeping company with - and although blackmail is an ugly word (as most thrillers say) it worked in this case. I was free to take the exams.

With just two days to go and about 150 things that I might have to answer questions on, I made the mistake of skimming over the surface of two thick medical and surgical textbooks and not swotting anything thoroughly. Examination day found me coldly resigned to my fate, there was no panic or nerves, I was devoid of all feeling. I went into the room like an automaton. With cold indifference I glanced at the question paper, then, with blank disbelief I looked again. Yes, there it was in black and white. 'Describe the signs and symptoms of acute appendicitis.' I gave an involuntary whoop of sheer delight and received a black look from the examiner, but now nothing else mattered. Surely the Gods were on my side. Weeks later I was among the proud number to receive my hospital badge from the Bishop of somewhere or other.

Of course, there was a party to celebrate the end of hospital finals. This was a reasonably sedate party in the lounge of the nurses quarters, attended by the Home Sister. There was a very moderate supply of sherry and under the watchful eye of the office sisters we endeavoured to relax and have fun, although it was rather refined fun. Promptly at 11pm the sisters suggested it was time for bed, reminding those of us who were working in the morning that we needed our beauty sleep. They then retired to their maidenly beds. That was the signal for the real party, it was held across the courtyard in the residents quarters. It was a pyjama party, a party that will live in the annals of hospital lore for generations to come. My recollections of the party as a whole are vague, but isolated incidents stand out, such as the distinctive taste of vodka and rough cider mixed, the singing of all 14 verses of the hospital song, 'Charity Charity universal.' Then, when all 14 verses had been sung the frantic racking of befuddled brains to think up some more, and finally of collapsing on my bed at 4am to snatch some sleep before early call at 5.30am.

In these advanced days when there is talk of an, 'automatic nurse,' device to record a patient's condition by remote control, one wonders what the nurse of the future will have to do. Already, with the introduction of medical clerks, or some such title, to take down a patient's particulars on admission, orderlies to do the dusting and menial chores that once fell to the nurse. Pre sterilised dressing packs, disposable transfusion sets and all the other recent labour saving devices, the nurses duties are becoming less and less. The pay, however is rising only slowly. In about 100 years from now the salary and conditions in the nursing profession might almost be inviting. While recent negotiations were in progress concerning nurses salaries, feeling was running high among the hard pressed student nurses. The hospital debating society chose it as a subject for one of their sessions. We invited the Assistant Matron and one of the Consultants to lead the discussion. All we got from the Assistant matron was the usual drivel about nursing being a calling, where we give of our best and expect nothing in return. That the gratitude of the patients, whom she pictured as being skilfully nursed back from the jaws of death, should be reward enough. The Consultant, Sir Lennox was subtle in his humour. He pointed out that whereas nursing had once been the most degrading of professions, fit only for the lowest women, it had now reached a peak of respectability. Acting, also, he pointed out had once been a despised profession followed by coarse and common people, and now everyone, from daughters of lords and ladies to shop girls, entertained dreams of becoming film stars. He closed with a smiling query as to what other disgusting professions would, in years to come, be accepted and even appraised by the public. The meeting broke up on this intriguing note, and although we had come to let off steam we went away entertained and strangely resigned. Nevertheless, most of us attended the march on the following weekend, carrying banners with the slogan, 'Pay us what we are worth.'

Nurses, by the very nature of their profession are required to be level headed and practical. Not given to gossip or superstition, one might say, but there is one superstition common among most nurses, especially of the old school. I came up against it again and again during my training. It is the mixing of red and white flowers in the same vase. I am not basically superstitious, but even seeing this in print makes me shudder, so deeply was it instilled in me during training. If ever some unsuspecting person put red and white flowers together in the same vase and put that vase in the ward, you could almost guarantee that there would be a death on the ward. This sounds like pure fantasy and allowing for all the usual arguments to the effect that death is not unusual in a hospital anyway, and that superstition is rubbish, it has been known to happen. Although, as I have said, I am not superstitious I would certainly not have red and white flowers on any ward of mine.

Another superstition common among nurses is that things happen in groups of three. Three births, three deaths and so on. It is strange, but this has often proved true, although it's a superstition I do not share. Nursing slang, like service slang, is a language all it's own. Frowned on by the Administrative Staff, it survives and prospers. A blood transfusion is a, 'drip,' a death is a, 'number 9.' The mortuary is the, 'ice box,' and so on. Further examples are unnecessary as it is largely understood only by those who use it.

Mondays and Thursdays were characterised by an unseemly rush to be first in the dining room. Not because there was any great treat on the menu - this only happened at Christmas - but because we had chips on those two days. Why the rush for chips, you may wonder. The chips, or saute' potatoes as they were called on the menu, were served up in ridiculous little silver covered dishes holding enough to feed about five people, and there were two dishes to a table. The tables seated up to thirty people. If you happened to be one of the last to arrive you had a choice of going without chips altogether, and making do with a soggy piece of ham for lunch or spending your lunch break at the dining table waiting for the second lot of chips. Early in our training Nurse Salter and I discovered that the only way to get properly fed was to purchase a paraffin lamp in lieu of a stove, and a frying pan. Every pay day we would tour the local supermarket for supplies of beans, spaghetti, tinned meat and whatever else would keep. Then, if we missed meals to keep important dates, we would not starve. This soon became known among the other girls on our corridor and the idea snowballed to an alarming extent. Within a matter of weeks there was hardly a room that didn't possess a stove and frying pan. Nurse Abraham, a thin lipped and shifty girl at the end of the corridor even went so far as to buy three frying pans and hire them out for a shilling an evening. This food racket went on for almost six months and finished in rather a dramatic way. In every class at school, college or university, in every group of people anywhere, there is always one person who is generally known as a duffer. It's easy to pick out this unfortunate being. Everything she does is wrong. If forty people were to climb a ladder and one were to fall, who would it be? Yes, the duffer. If a group went to watch swans on a lake, who would fall in? The duffer. On an excursion, who would miss the train back? The duffer. So it was with Nurse Heenan. Connie Heenan had rushed with great enthusiasm into the cooking craze. She had stocked her locker with all manner of foods. Not content with mere tins, she bought bacon, eggs by the dozen, and one fateful day, a packet of kippers. It was late in the evening, when the Home Sister was making her goodnight round. She stopped on C corridor, sniffed, and, unbelieving, she sniffed again. Meanwhile, in Connie's room a small party was in progress. Four of us were sat around on the bed and on the floor, and Connie was busily engaged in frying the kippers over a single quivering candle flame, (she had forgotten to get any paraffin for the stove). The room was dense with smoke and kipper fumes when the door burst open and in stormed the Home Sister.

I shall never forget the look on her face, a mixture of anguish, amazement and pure disbelief. She stood for two or three seconds, with her jaws moving trying to summon up speech, then finally in a strangled voice, she said. "See me tomorrow in my office," and stumbled away down the corridor. There was a pregnant silence in the little room. "Does she mean all of us?" Connie piped up. Somehow the party spirit had left us and we forced down the kippers without enjoyment. The next morning found us waiting with trepidation outside Sister's door. She must have cooled off during the night, because she was quite reasonable. Of course, she pointed out the dangers of fire, damage to hospital property, and of keeping food in a heated room without a refrigerator. Then came the bit about having adequate meals provided in the dining room. We at least managed to get in a word in about the poor quality of hospital food. We were sent back to the Nurses Home with a solemn promise never to do such stupid things again. There is not much honour among student nurses, so nobody parted with their frying pans except, of course, poor Connie. It was on hire from Nurse Abrahams, too.

There was a sewing machine in the nurses home, and from time to time an epidemic of dressmaking would break out. It was during one of these that somebody suggested we should make a dress form. Over the weeks four or five of the girls had been taking packets of Plaster of Paris from casualty until we thought we had enough to make a dress form. The next big question, who would be the model? Well! Who else but Connie, she wouldn't refuse, good old Connie. We all gathered in her room with rolls of bandage, Plaster of Paris, bowls of water, and ingenious stroke - a pair of plaster cutters. Luckily, Connie was very slight, so we reckoned that with the extra inches of plaster the dress form when completed would measure 36, 24, 36. Roughly the same measurement of the four conspirators. Mollie Ryde, the efficient one among us, who was later to take the gold medal and Matron's prize, made an expert job of the plaster cast. We mounted it on some hardboard, and got one of the porters to make a stand out of three broom handles. Proudly we carted it down to the sewing room in the basement. It did useful service there for three months until someone from the hospital board of governors was doing a tour with Matron. There were three of us fitting a fabulous evening gown on to the dress form when in walked Matron and this important looking gentleman. "I say, Matron," he remarked. "An ingenious device, what." He came closer to have a look. "What's it made of?" He queried. Of course, it had to be Connie who answered. "Plaster of Paris, sir," she squeaked. This seemed to amuse him a great deal, though nobody dared to look to see Matron's reaction. We fully expected someone to come and take the model to use for bandaging practise in the practical room after that, but nothing further was said.

Bedpan washers are, I believe, standard equipment in most hospitals. This was not the case a few years ago. One of the first bedpan washers ever, was the proud property of Harper Ward. We had it for a trial period of six months. People came from all over the hospital just to see it in action. It was a gigantic affair and worked on a similar principle to the modern dishwashing machine. You put the bedpan in the machine and pressed a button. There was a great metallic clanking sound, a red light went on and all sorts of other sounds issued forth. When the green light went on it was safe to open the door and remove the bedpan. Safe, that was, if the operator realised that the bedpan would be red hot from the boiling water in the machine. There were no end of burnt fingers until Sister put up a notice directly over the green button. "Nurses will wait at least ten minutes before opening the door, to allow the receptacle to cool." She obviously thought the word, 'bedpan,' sounded common.

This system worked well when there was just the isolated bedpan but when we had six or seven at a time, only one could be washed in the machine and we had to resort to crude old fashioned methods to wash the others. I was doing dressings on Harper Ward when a frightful squealing sound came from the direction of the sluice. Leaving my patient with her stitches exposed to the germ laden air, I rushed to investigate. There was Connie, her hands to her face standing paralysed while a jet of water streamed from the bedpan washer all over her. She stood there dripping, with little puddles forming around her feet. It seemed she had not shut the door properly and the thing shot open almost drowning her. Fortunately it was cold water, not yet hot.

Treatment of psychiatric patients through the medium of the gramophone was a little known field of therapy. It was being pioneered in the hospital where I did the psychiatric part of my general training. We had as a patient a middle aged business man, Mr Avery. He had got tied up with business worries and been working late into the night for years without proper meals and no relaxation. Eventually the strain proved too great and he suffered a complete mental breakdown. It was a long job and he wasn't responding to the prescribed drugs. The main feature of his case was a complete inability to relax. The Consultant Psychiatrist was extremely interested in hypnosis as a means of inducing complete relaxation, and was the author of a number of articles on the subject. In the student rounds one morning Professor Donaldson was expounding on his pet theme when one of the students posed an interesting question. Was it possible to hypnotise a patient with a recorded voice when the speaker was absent? "That's an extremely good question," the Professor beamed. "I shall provide you with an answer next week." At the end of the round the Prof didn't stay for coffee in Sister's office, as was his usual custom, but went hurrying down the ward. "I expect he's gone to borrow a tape recorder," grinned the student. He was joking, but his words proved true. The next week, on the round, he reminded the students of the question posed the previous week. "Now gentlemen," he began. "I have here a recording of a session of hypnosis which I held in my clinic on the weekend. I have played this recording back to several volunteer patients, with little success so far. However, It would seem that for hypnosis to be effective the operator must be present," and here he paused. "It has given me the idea for a new type of relaxation therapy, which I intend to try out on Mr Avery, with his permission, of course." Mr Avery had refused treatment by hypnosis, and as he was not responding to sedative drugs, Professor Donaldson had resigned himself to a long and difficult illness. It was arranged that a nurse should sit with Mr Avery in a comfortable sitting room and record his reactions, and degree of relaxation while the tape was being played. Sister thought it would be good experience for one of the 'general' nurses so I was chosen for the job. The sitting room was cosily furnished, a warm looking gas fire glowed and the lights were just right, not too harsh. We were to sit comfortably by the fire while the tape was being played. The voice was persuasive. "You are heavy and tired," it began in a soothing tone. I settled more comfortably in the chair and closed my eyes, listening to the voice. I was brought down to earth sharply by Mr Avery shaking my shoulder. "The tape's finished, nurse," he said. I started up, embarrassed. "You've been asleep for half an hour," he laughed. That was the first time anyone had heard Mr Avery laugh for more than two months. Strangely enough, from then on he seemed to pick up. Prof Donaldson maintained that it was the relaxation therapy that helped his cure. I say it was because he found that he was able to laugh again.

In these beauty conscious days, mechanical things like electric curling tongs, eyelash curlers, and even electric toothbrushes are taken for granted. The sight of them is not unusual. When I started my training (and this may date me) the sight of an eyelash curling appliance was rare. So rare, indeed, that no one knew what it was. One evening while we were in the preliminary training school, I wandered in to nurse Miles room for a natter and saw the weirdest contraption on her dressing table. It resembled a pair of scissors but instead of blades it had two parallel bent bars going crosswise from the middle. Thinking it was some kind of surgical instrument, I enquired what it was doing on Joan's dressing table. "Oh, that thing, it's an eyelash curler," she told me and proceeded to give me a demonstration of how it worked. There was a kick at the door and Heather Baines came in, laden with rollers, hair lacquer, setting lotion and about half a dozen brands of face cream. They were going to have a beauty evening. I went off to get all my lotions and lacquers and the three of us set about experimenting with our faces. Gradually the talk got around to that day's lectures and the problem of learning all the theatre trolleys and remembering all the instruments. "Hmmph," scoffed Joan, "I don't believe that even Sister tutor knows all the instruments, why, there are literally hundreds of them." Then Heather hit on the brilliant idea of putting the eye lash curlers in the instrument cupboard to see if any of the Sisters knew what they were. We rushed at once down to the lecture room, only to find the instrument cupboard locked. Of course, Sister tutor always kept the key. This presented a new problem, how to get the eyelash curlers into the cupboard without anyone in authority seeing the manoeuvre, and thus spoiling it all.

During the practical session next day, Heather offered to clean out the cupboard, and a rather surprised Sister gave her the keys. The deed was accomplished. It only remained for the fun to start. It didn't take long for the whole PTS to learn about it and we waited with baited breath for someone in authority to notice the curlers. No one did. During one of the practical sessions Heather (it was always Heather) asked Sister Tutor to go through the instruments with her. This aroused a lot of interest in the other members of the class, and soon a little crowd was standing around. She had gone about halfway through the cupboard when she picked up the eyelash curlers. "A nasal speculum," she said quite calmly, and didn't seem to notice the suppressed gasp we gave. Of course, at the next practical session we asked Sister Rogers, the clinical instructor to go through the instruments. She was nearer the mark. An eyelid retractor, was her verdict. We could hardly believe it. Nurses in preliminary training school are always given the impression that a trained nurse is infallible whether she be Sister, Staff Nurse, or Matron. Being young and impressionable and without the cynicism that tends to come later, we believed this myth. It was, in fact, the Senior Consultant Surgeon that rumbled us, as the saying is. He came up to lecture us on surgical techniques and illustrated his talk with the various surgical instruments involved. We were at a practical session when he came in, and crossed to the instrument cupboard. Obviously, he was going to select the instruments for the lecture that would follow. We were a bit apprehensive as he rummaged through the shelves but he went without saying anything. The next lecture was about modern techniques in abdominal surgery, and was ably delivered. In a brief summary at the end of the lecture he held up the instruments one by one and explained their uses. Last of all, and much to our amazement, he held up the notorious foreigner from the cupboard. "One 'outdoor girl,' eyelash curlers, as used by my two teenage daughters, and no earthly use in any instrument cupboard," he stated.

Another highlight of the preliminary training school was the photographer's visit. We all had a passport type photograph taken which was never shown to us but was stuck in a file in Matron's office together with a record of all our doings, good or bad, throughout our training. Heather swore that she would put on her most moronic expression for this photograph. As we never saw it we were left wondering if she ever did.

Wherever nurses gather together there are grumbles about nursing conditions. Poor pay, long hours and such things, but taking a broad view, conditions are improving. Slower, maybe than most professions, but nevertheless, improving. Sister Overton, the old stalwart of E.N.T, used to often remark on the appalling conditions when she trained, especially if one of the girls wanted her off duty changed or a weekend off. "When I trained, my girl," she would say, "There was no such thing as a weekend off, I got half a day a month, and if we had a few emergencies I wouldn't even get that. There was none of this coming back late from meals if you had left the ward late. We had all our meals in the ward kitchen, often standing up to eat them. The same food that the patients ate, and the nurses cooked it, too. There were no domestics in those days, the nurses did the scrubbing and the cleaning as well as run errands, make tea and clean the ward sister's shoes." (we didn't believe this last bit). "Do you realise, nurse, that the very uniform you wear is traditionally styled as that of a lower servant, and Matron's dress styled as a Victorian housekeeper."

Of course, Sister Overton was a good sort, and after all this twaddle she would throw her hands up and shout. "Alright, take the weekend off, you're no use here anyway," and the nurse concerned would scuttle away before she changed her mind. The nursing profession has grown from an extremely disreputable beginning. Originally there were no trained nurses, and no trained doctors either. There was usually an old hag in each little village who acted as a 'witch doctor', layer out, midwife and general adviser. She was often a drunkard but the superstitious village folk respected and feared her. In pre Victorian times the lowest profession was prostitution, and nursing came a close second. Many older country doctors will tell how, when they first started practising, the village midwives were very much against them and did all in their power to turn the people against them, too. There was a deep rooted suspicion of drugs and medicines except, of course, herbal remedies used by the local midwives.

When the nervous young GP was conducting a delivery, there would be all the old women of the village crowding into the bedroom to make sure that he did it correctly. There was no such thing as sterility, the presence of micro organisms was not even suspected until much later. More often than not, the mother had a normal delivery, only to succumb in two or three days to, 'child bed fever,' or puerperal sepsis. At Crimea, Florence Nightingale did much to improve conditions for the wounded and sick soldiers. She worked ceaselessly to bring cleanliness and ventilation, and above all, a good standard of nursing to the troops. Although Florence Nightingale was a leader among women and, indeed, a truly great woman, she was not liked by her nurses. To revolutionise the conditions prevalent in that day she had to have a forceful personality, and such a personality is by no means a popular one. She literally bullied everyone until they came up to her standards. Yes, the lady with the lamp was far more likely to be doing a round to check on the efficiency of her nurses than to comfort the wounded soldiers. The modern nurse is completely spoiled when compared to her predecessors. There are ward clerks to take the burden of paperwork from the nurses shoulders, and there are technicians responsible for the smooth running of all machinery. A few years ago the nurses had to oil all the mechanical devices on the ward. Domestic staff are employed to do the sweeping and dusting. There is a soiled linen service, where nurses merely empty the badly soiled linen into a container and it is collected by a van and returned shining white. There is a central sterile supplies depot, which deals with all the syringes and instruments. Nurses don't even have to test urine with five or six bottles of chemicals any more. A medical firm has made little tablets or impregnated sticks which show up anything abnormal when a few drops of urine are dropped on to them.

With all these improvements the outsider may be tempted to ask. "Well, what does the nurse do?" She works a 42 hour week, I repeat, works. There will never be a substitute for giving bedpans, doing dressings and a thousand and one other duties. The latest idea from America is closed circuit television within the wards so that the nurse can press a button and see how her patient is progressing at the other end of the ward. One is tempted to wonder if the next step will be robot nurses. Well, they said space travel was impossible.

Chapter 7

Two of the highlights in the hospital where I trained were the secondment for a period of three months to a specialist hospital some miles away. This helped to break the long period spent at the main hospital, provided a change of scenery and the stimulating effects of new faces. My three months at a hospital for infectious diseases were hilarious. The discipline was so relaxed as to be practically non existent, yet there was a happy atmosphere.

Roger, a young man of about twentyfive, had been in for four months trying to get jaundice out of his system. He felt quite well, and often said it was about time they let him out. The doctors thought otherwise though as he was still infectious and a potential danger to others. To pass the time he would compose ridiculous lyrics about all members of staff and send anonymous love letters to the Ward Sister containing such corny phrases as, 'your eyes have enchanted me,' or, 'your smile melts my heart.' Sister had a shrewd suspicion where they came from, but took it all in good part. Some of the meaner nurses on the ward said that they were about the only love letters she had ever had. There was a choice of two hospitals in which to do our three months fever nursing. One was a little country village a few miles out of town, and the other was some twentyfive miles away. One would think that the hospital farthest away would get more of our nurses because, firstly, it was a seaside place and secondly it offered a complete break with the mother hospital. This was not the case, however. The little hospital nearer home employed male nurses, consequently, it got seven out of every ten of our girls. One of the male nurses was a rough, much travelled Scot - Jock, of course. Why he had ever chosen nursing no one ever knew. Apart from the fact that the pay is not enough for a man to support a family, he seemed entirely unsuited to the career. He was a typical dour Scot, even to the point of appearing brusque. He seldom smiled and spoke only in monosyllables. There was a severe epidemic of measles while I was at the fever hospital. It was a mutation of the usual measles virus and bronchial complications were frequent. Being the only fever hospital within a twentyfive mile radius all the seriously ill cases came to our wards. For once the children's ward was full. Here we noticed the change in Jock. He was a different person. All day he spent in the children's ward, whether he was on duty or not. He would bring comics and soft toys for the children and would smuggle sweets into the ward. The convalescent children would all gather round while Jock knocked up a puppet show from some old bits of wood and coloured paper. He was something of an amateur conjuror, too and would entertain us for hours and would end up by producing bars of chocolate from nowhere, and coins from thin air. The children loved him and soon discovered that he had a vast store of adventure stories to tell. He had travelled widely and could conjure up stories at a minutes notice of shipwrecks, volcanoes, earthquakes or anything else that the children demanded. The change in Jock was so noticeable that word of it finally got round to Matron's office, and he was put on the Children's

Ward permanently, an arrangement which suited everybody.

Another of the male nurses was Andy, a tall gangly lad. He was very popular with the nurses. If ever there was a nurse not in her quarters by midnight, it was a fair guess that she was out with Andy. He had no respect for rules whatsoever. He managed to talk his way out of all his escapades. Though Andy was the kind of person who could get away with anything, it had to be him who went down with chicken pox while working on the Children's Ward. He came on duty one morning more subdued than usual and said he wasn't feeling too good. Nobody took much notice. About halfway through the morning he noticed one or two spots on his arm, but still, nobody thought any more about it. Visiting time came and Andy was chatting to the mother of one of the children. She noticed the spots and said they were chicken pox spots. Andy, quite alarmed, went in search of Sister. "Rubbish." She exclaimed on seeing the spots "Of course it's not chicken pox, it's just a few heat bumps". The child's mother, on hearing this merely put on a knowing look. "Four kids, I've reared, and they all had chicken pox together - I'm telling you my boy. Them's chicken pox spots," When the Houseman came around Andy immediately collared him. "Hey, what are these spots?" "Syphilis, probably," grinned the Houseman, then, on close inspection he said he thought they were gnat bites. The next morning Andy came on duty, he was still looking off colour and had one or two more spots. Everyone was treating it as a big joke. Being Andy, they thought he was trying to find a way to get off work. As the day wore on he became flushed and complained of nausea and headache. Someone hit on the bright idea of taking his temperature. It was 102. He was sent over to sick quarters. When he removed his shirt for the doctor's examination he found his back was covered in typical chicken pox spots. The mother was triumphant, she searched out Sister just to say, "I told you so."

There was a little coloured boy on Children's ward. He had come in with paratyphoid fever and was quite ill for a while. His mother visited him every day, she would say to us, "Bobby's flushed today, nurse," or, "Bobby's pale," but we could never see the difference. To our inexperienced eyes he always looked coal black. Of course, we could tell his condition by his temperature and pulse rate, but as far as the condition of his skin was concerned, unless he was actually perspiring we couldn't tell anything. One of the girls brought the subject up at the next clinical lecture. She wanted to know if it was possible to make any observations about the skin colour of a West Indian or African patient. This led to an open discussion. How can you tell if he's cyanosed, asked Mary Wayne. The tutor said that it was a matter of experience, and only by nursing coloured people for months on end, could the nurse begin to observe changes in their colour. "Nurse them until you are completely familiar with the normal," he observed, "and you will recognise the abnormal at a glance."

Years ago, when there was no television, films or radio, the travelling circus was an important annual event for the village people. Nowadays most fairgrounds contain only a few bingo stalls, a rifle range, rides for the kiddies, roll a penny tables and maybe a gypsy fortune teller. In the days when people flocked from far and near to see the fair there was a much better show. For example, where in these enlightened days would we see a circus fat lady, dwarfs, a giant, maybe, or a bearded lady? These celebrities are extremely rare except in one place. The outpatients department of a hospital. Yes, with the advances in surgery and medicine in the last twenty years, folk with these conditions are seen less and less.

Mike Alton was a giant. Not just a big man, but a giant. He was naturally a tall fellow, some six feet seven inches, but it wasn't his height that made him a giant. It was the immense size of his features, his hands and feet. He came to Morgan Ward for hormone therapy. His was a strange story. Until two years ago he had been a normal person. Tall, maybe, but not out of the ordinary, yet now he was striking in appearance. How did these changes occur? What disease was it that could change a normal young man into a spectacle in just a few years? Mike was admitted to the ward and investigations were started to determine the cause of his rapidly increasing size. It was discovered that he had a rare tumour of the pituitary gland. This was secreting large amounts of the growth hormone found in the anterior lobe of the gland. Consequently Mike was getting more and more terrifying in appearance. Eventually, of course - and this used to happen before surgeons dared to advance into the brain, - the build up of intracranial pressure caused by the enlarging tumour would have proved fatal. The surgeons decided to operate to remove the tumour, a hazardous and risky operation. The pituitary gland is about the size of a dried pea, and is situated deep in the base of the brain. Mike was scheduled for theatre on Monday morning. He had had a long talk with the surgeon who was operating on him and he realised the risk involved. He was quite jovial right up until the trolley came to wheel him to theatre. Maybe a little too cheerful, we thought. This is often the case with male patients. A man has been brought up in the belief that it is unmanly to show fear, and Englishmen especially are indoctrinated from their schooldays to keep a 'stiff upper lip'. Women, on the other hand, are not in the least ashamed to admit that they are afraid. It has been observed that women, in general, have less immediate after effects from anaesthetic than men. Could this be because they have not suppressed their feelings of fear and as a result, have no build up of tension within them when they are coming round? Or maybe it's not as simple as that. We will leave the point open to debate.

Mike was in theatre for about five hours. Theatre rang through for a nurse to take him back to the ward early that afternoon and Mary Blythe, a junior, went to fetch him. We got him into bed with the help of two burly theatre porters, left Mary to 'special' him and carried on with the ward work. As he regained consciousness Mike began to get very restless, tossing from side to side and throwing the bedclothes about. Mary Blythe was only five feet two inches in her shoes, so she found it extremely difficult to hold him. In the end she had to summon two other nurses to hold him down while the third one rushed to get some cot sides. We fixed these around the bed and with the help of a sedative injection peace was restored. Mike made a good recovery after that first day, and was soon able to sit out of bed in an arm chair. Although nothing could be done to make his grossly enlarged features more normal, the tumour had been removed and he was assured of at least a normal life span. Less than a century ago the story would have had a choice of two endings. If he had belonged to a rich family he would have been hidden away in an attic and been nursed for the remaining few years of his life. If he had been poor, he would probably have finished up in a travelling circus until ill health caught up with him and he would have died in the poor house or the gutter.

At the other end of the scale, but no less tragic, there is the dwarf. There was one admitted to Harper Ward with an inguinal hernia. The operation was performed and he made an uneventful recovery. It was in the follow up clinic, some six weeks later, that the subject of his dwarfism was brought up. It appeared that his condition had never been investigated. The Surgeon asked him if he would agree to come to the Medical Ward and have some tests done to investigate the cause. Mr Jones readily agreed and some weeks later he was admitted. It was ascertained that he, too, was suffering from a tumour of the anterior lobe of the pituitary gland. In Mr Jones's case, the tumour had a depressant effect on the production of the growth hormone. An operation was performed and the tumour removed. There was no increase in his size as the bones had already finished growing. A bone grafting operation was mentioned, but Mr Jones made it clear that he was quite content as he was, and had no desire to be, 'got at,' by the surgeons, as he put it. The operation would have probably meant grafting some new bone on to his thigh bones to give him a few extra inches in height. Even today it is not an operation that is usually performed unless the patient expressly desires it, and all the circumstances are favourable.

The only operation I have seen performed for cosmetic reasons was performed on a young girl of twenty one. Shiela was an extremely pretty girl, but she had one drawback, she was over six feet tall. Consequently she stooped and was overly self conscious. She had been referred to our Orthopaedic Wards from a psychiatric clinic. She was very depressed and felt she was a freak. Her case history went back six years. As a teenager she was subject to fits of black depression. Not just teenage moods, but almost suicidal despair. The reason was obvious. A young man who is tall is often seen to stoop and be a bit self conscious about his height, but, how much worse is it in a young woman. She wouldn't go out dancing because she was invariably taller than her partners and lately she had grown so self conscious that she would stay in the house except for essential journeys. When the psychiatrist, after having checked with the orthopaedic surgeon, suggested that there might be an operation or a series of operations to correct the problem, Shiela was delighted. She didn't mind any operation or inconvenience as long as it made her more like other girls of her own age. She was admitted to Mason Ward and an operation performed whereby the surgeon took three inches off her height. With a special saw he cut a piece out of each thigh bone, somewhere near the centre, and joined the ends.

Theoretically this sounds simple, but it is a long and hazardous operation. Shiela had to lie in bed with her legs immobilised for weeks, then there was daily physiotherapy to prevent wasting of the muscles. At last the day came when she was allowed to stand up. It was a very weak and wobbly Shiela who stood before the mirror assisted by Sister, Staff Nurse and two crutches. It was a delight to see her face. Although there was a long period of convalescence ahead of her, learning to walk again, she could see the difference in her height. She determined to be up and about and going to dances in record time. A clever move on the part of the Surgeon was to assign her case history and follow up to a senior medical student, a massive fellow of six feet four. How nice it would be to report that he married her and they lived happily ever after, but he didn't.

Another fair ground attraction was the bearded lady. This unfortunate woman was sure to draw the crowds a few decades ago. Her beard would range from a scant growth of hair on her chin and upper lip to a full bushy beard. In the days before the development of electrolysis, such a woman had no alternative but to shave every day. This was by no means satisfactory as it resulted in a coarser texture of the skin, and sometimes five o clock shadow. There was no effective treatment as the drugs in use today were not even thought of then. Hirsutism, or hairyness in a woman can be caused by two or three different diseases, the most common one being some kind of tumour of the supra-renal glands. It can be treated by operation or by hormone therapy and good results are usually obtained.

The circus fat lady, too, was another big attraction. Their condition was usually due to a glandular imbalance. Some of these fat ladies weighed anything up to 42 stones. Usually they didn't live long owing to the tremendous strain on the heart of carrying around such a weight. Many diseases can be recognised at a glance by certain characteristic features, colour, facial expression, or smell. The following chapter deals with a few of these.

Chapter 8

Graves disease, or toxic goitre can be recognised at once by the nurse or doctor. The main diagnostic feature is exophthalmos, or popping eyes. Some of these patients look really frightening and their eyes bulge to such an extent that it is only with great difficulty they can close the lids.

Mrs Ryan was admitted to Eddison Ward for treatment of thyrotoxicosis. She was a classic example of the disease. Her eyes were almost bulging from her head. It is a frightening experience to walk down the ward on night duty and see one of these patients. They look startling in broad daylight, but in a dimly lit ward the effect is shattering. Nurse Hampton was doing her first spell of nights, she had only been nursing for six months and was still at the stage where she believed everything she was told. In the night nurses sitting room the conversation got around to Miller Ward and the mysterious noises that could be heard from time to time. One of the

Housemen had found his way into the sitting room which, of course was strictly against the rules. He was livening up the conversation with the weirdest stories of his experiences on nights. Those of us who had been nursing longer knew this to be a complete fabrication. The only times Housemen appear on the wards at night are for emergencies, and certainly they have no time for sitting around waiting for ghosts to appear. Anyway, Nurse Hampton didn't know this and she was sitting, open mouthed, taking in every word. When she got back to the Ward she was extremely jumpy. She had been sitting at the ward desk afraid to make a tour of the patients, when she heard shuffling footsteps behind her. Hardly daring to breathe she turned her head then, patients forgotten, she let out one loud shout and ran stumbling out into the Ward kitchen. Nurse Manning, her senior, returning from supper found her huddled in a frightened heap. On going to investigate Nurse Manning found half of the Ward awake and Mrs Ryan sobbing her heart out by her bed. "I didn't mean to frighten the child." She said between sniffs. "I just got up to ask if there was a cup of tea going." A cup of tea was inevitable now that everyone was awake. Nurse Hampton could laugh about it in the clear light of the next morning, but she has never liked night duty since.

Anyone who has ever worked with cancer patients will agree that it is recognisable by its smell. It is a kind of musty smell. Not very marked in the individual, but noticeable as one walks in to a ward full of these patients. In the last decade the percentage of complete cures for cancer patients has gone up considerably. Nowadays, with everything possible being done to inform the public about the disease, with mobile cancer detection clinics being pioneered and revolutionary methods of treatment, it is more than halfway to being beaten. Mrs Roberts was normally a robust healthy woman but for eighteen months she had been troubled by vague stomach pain and intermittent bouts of diarrhoea. Her family doctor diagnosed colitis, an inflammation of the small intestine, and had been treating her accordingly. The treatment had given no relief and after repeated visits he referred her to our outpatients clinic. It is usual for a nurse to chaperone all examinations of female patients. Occasionally one hears of a case where a woman patient accuses the doctor of unprofessional behaviour. These are often found to be hysterical young women or maladjusted spinsters. Anyway, our training school believed in safety first, so we chaperoned. After the patient had gone the doctor called me to one side. "Well, nurse, what would you diagnose there?" he asked. "Colitis, I suppose," I replied, "all the signs and symptoms point that way." "No, nurse, I think you will find you are wrong, unless I am much mistaken we have a case of carcinoma of the colon on our hands." I was surprised to say the least. "But she doesn't look like a cancer patient," I protested. "Maybe not, but she smells like one," he replied. "We will see what the microscope says," and with that he handed me some slides for labelling. A few days later the pathological report came back. He was right, and Mrs Roberts was put on the waiting list for surgery. She was admitted a little while later and a laparotomy was performed. The surgeon cut away the affected length of intestine and joined up the two ends. Mrs Roberts returned to the ward, where she made a good recovery. She was up and about in less than a week, and out of hospital in three weeks. That was five years ago and there has been no recurrence of her symptoms since. Her case is one of many such success stories.

There are certain diseases of the facial nerves that have characteristic expressions. A familiar one is Myasthenia Gravis. The patients have a kind of grimacing expression or 'snarling smile' as some books describe it. Myasthenia Gravis includes the muscles of the shoulder causing weakness of the arms and sometimes the leg muscles. It is caused by a debility of the muscles, they tire quickly consequently the facial expression is less marked in the morning, after rest and more noticeable in the evening, after a long day.

Everyone knows the features of the Downs syndrome child. There is a similarity about all of them. There is a basic fault in the structure of the body cells that is one of the characteristics of all these children. They are usually happy, affectionate children and very lovable. Facial paralysis or Bell's

Palsy is another disease that can be recognised at a glance. The patient, when asked to smile, smiles with one side of his face only. When asked to blink, can only blink with one eye. Facial paralysis can be caused by inflammation of the facial nerve from exposure to cold, or at birth from a long and difficult delivery using forceps. It usually clears up in time, but it is extremely distressing for the person concerned.

Obstructive jaundice can be diagnosed at a glance. The patient is a deep yellow colour, especially the whites of the eyes. It can be caused by blockage of the common bile duct, a gall stone, for example. The bile cannot escape through the usual channel and is absorbed into the blood stream giving rise to the peculiar deep yellow colour. Tom Fenton was a merchant seaman. He had been admitted via casualty complaining of severe abdominal pain. He was settled into bed and the Houseman came to examine him. This was somewhere around midnight and a hasty diagnosis of appendicitis was made. There seemed to be no immediate danger of perforation so he was left under observation until the morning. He had been a normal colour on admission, but the next morning Sister thought there was a slight yellowish tinge to his skin although no one else could see it. As the day wore on, Tom became more and more yellow. When the Consultant came to do his rounds the Houseman was with him. ,Ah! The new arrival, I presume" the Consultant, Mr Barnes remarked. "What have you diagnosed?" he demanded of the Houseman who was showing signs of discomfiture. "Come along, come along. Let's see the chart." The Houseman weakly handed it over. Barnes face was a study, "Perhaps (he said sarcastically) you would like to explain to the students the anatomical connection between acute appendicitis and obstructive jaundice." Tom Fenton spoke up for the bewildered Houseman. "It's all right, chum," he grinned, winking at the consultant, "I wasn't yeller last night."

Mrs Wright was brought into casualty in a deep coma. Her skin was dry and hot and her eyes were sunken. There were four student nurses on casualty at this time, and as we were not very busy,

Sister called us in to make a diagnosis as to the cause of this coma. We went through all the possibilities and grew more and more puzzled. It wasn't likely to be a stroke, Nurse Edwards said, because the patient was too young. There was no paralysis, no neurological signs except, of course, the coma. Nurse Hampton, the dramatic one, diagnosed a brain tumour but was quickly shouted down. Sister came in eventually to see what we had decided. We said it was either cerebral compression, stroke, or cerebral tumour. "Oh my! You do choose the unusual things," she laughed. "Now, did anyone notice the smell of pear drops coming from this patient?" Yes, of course, now that Sister had mentioned it, it was quite noticeable. "Now there are three kinds of coma that can be recognised by the smell of the patient's breath. One is alcoholic coma, or the, 'dead drunk,' The other is uraemia, where there is a strong offensive smell to the breath. And the other is diabetic coma where the breath smells of acetone or pear drops," she stated.

The peculiar smell of the breath in a case of diabetic coma is due to the fact that acetone, or ketones, is a by product of fat metabolism. Incidentally, if you are dieting drastically to lose some weight, and you realise that your breath smells of pear drops, you have probably dieted too much! In diabetes mellitus the body is unable to process carbohydrates or sugars. The sugar is excreted in the patient's urine and the carbohydrates cannot be used for energy. The body burns up its own fat for energy instead of carbohydrates which it cannot break down without insulin. This smell is also noticed in cases of starvation.

Parkinsons disease can be recognised at a glance by the look of the patient. He often has a slightly vacant expression due to weakness of the facial muscles although there us no impairment of intelligence. He walks with a characteristic shuffling gait and his fingers are constantly moving in a 'pill rolling' movement.

There were two Medical Consultants on Morgan Ward. It was a big ward and was usually very busy. The two consultants, Mr Emery and Mr Docherty usually had conflicting opinions on practically everything. Sister Yeoman usually managed to act as a peacemaker. Mr Emery's round was on a Monday morning and Mr Docherty was on a Thursday. Sister Yeoman had a ruling passion that everything had to be in apple pie order for the rounds. She usually stayed on duty to conduct them herself. For hours before a round she would flap up and down the Ward chivvying the nurses and generally picking holes in everything. Nurse Hampton was on duty on Monday morning. It was particularly busy. Sister Yeoman was up and down the Ward organising everybody, two new patients had just been admitted and the work was piling up. To distinguish their various patients, the two surgeons had their names printed on slips of paper in large black capital letters. These they stuck on their respective patient's beds. One of the new patients was for Mr Emery and the other was for Mr Docherty. One was a cerebral haemorrhage and the other was a coronary thrombosis. Nurse Hampton stuck the label on each chart just as Mr Emery and his following of medical students began the round, Sister Yeoman bringing up the rear. All went smoothly until he came to the coronary thrombosis.

"Sister," he yelled, "This belongs to Mr Docherty, remove my label at once," with a withering glance at the patient, who was unconscious anyway, he continued on down the Ward. He came eventually to the cerebral haemorrhage. This unfortunate soul had, of course, Mr Docherty's label on his bed. Again the roaring shout. "Sister!" poor Sister Yeoman was reduced by this time to a jittering wreck. "Who placed the ultimate sentence on this miserable gentleman by placing him in Docherty's care when he should have been in mine?" he demanded. "Kindly label him correctly. Gentlemen, let us proceed." And so the round ended. Mr Emery habitually adjourned to Sister's office for coffee after his rounds. By the time Sister was free again to go in search of Nurse Hampton, Staff nurse had sent her off duty. It was her day off the next day so Staff nurse thought it better to get her out of the way until Sisters anger had subsided a little.

Psychiatrists are well aware of the power the human mind possesses to bury unpleasant events deep in the subconscious. Commonplace examples of this are found in the occurrence of amnesia after a serious accident. The amnesia frequently goes back to just before the accident. This is nature's way of blotting out what might otherwise be a disturbing memory. Labour amnesia, too is fairly common, where a mother can remember the joy of holding her newborn baby, but the memory of the contractions leading up to the birth is often only a vague blur. The six weeks I spent on Frazer Ward were, I think, the most unpleasant weeks in the whole of my training. The Sister was one of the old school. A veritable dragon. Everything had to be perfect on the Ward. Drugs had to be given right on the minute they were due. There was no room for inefficiency. I got off to a bad start when I forgot to regulate old Mr Halton's drip and he got a whole bottle of plasma in about half an hour. After that nothing I did was right. Every morning, coming on duty, Sister had a little list of things I hadn't done or had done wrong. She would walk around behind me, picking out anything that wasn't right. Obviously, knowing this made me more nervous than I would normally be, and I did some silly things. It was a kind of vicious circle with me in the centre. In those six weeks I came nearer to finishing with Hospital life than ever in my training. Every other day I would write out my notice, only to be persuaded by some of the other girls that that it was only a phase, and that there was no sense in being bullied into resigning just because I thought I was being victimised by Sister.

Eventually my six weeks on the ward expired, and it was with a great sense of relief that I saw my name on the notice board for Outpatients department. Although I can remember most of the girls I trained with, and all of the wards and their respective Sisters, I can never remember the name of that Sister on Frazer Ward. I have tried time and time again to remember it, but it just will not come to mind. I am sure this is a case of my subconscious mind not wanting to remember.

My time on outpatients was much more enjoyable. Sister Newbold was a homely Scotswoman. She was quiet and efficient, and above all, she was kind. She had a knack of putting people at their ease and her department always ran smoothly with no apparent effort. Nettie Newbold, as she was known, was one of those women whom nothing on earth could disturb. No matter how busy the clinic, no matter how long the list of casualties, no matter how irritable the Consultants were, old Nettie stood calm and unflappable. She had a great love of flowers and there were always vases of them scattered all over the department. There was a grateful ex patient who owned a large garden and every Monday a large basket full of flowers would arrive for her. She was very particular about the care of these, and would appoint a nurse to change the water in the vases regularly. If the flowers failed to last until the following Monday Nettie would have the nurse in her office and cross examine her to see if she really had been changing the water.

One morning in the middle of a very busy outpatients clinic, an odd looking man came up. "Hey, are you the Sister?" he enquired. I replied that he would find Sister in her office. "Well, it aint Sister that I want, really," he said, "It's that young doctor." "Do you have an appointment?" I asked. "Oh no," he laughed. "We'm old friends, me and the Doc." "We are very busy," I began as politely as possible, "if you will leave your name, and tell me which doctor it is I will pass on your regards." "Oh, 'Arry Rags, that's the doctor," he was laughing openly now, I suspected that he was just pulling my leg but there was an element of doubt, so I daren't shout him out. He had been talking all the time in a loud voice and had attracted the attention of a group of patients waiting for their appointments. Suddenly the door opened and an irate Doctor poked his head out, Nurse," he began, "I've been ringing for the last five minutes, can't you hear the buzzer?" Then he caught sight of the man. "Oh, hello, Tom. Are you causing trouble again?" he said cordially, and gave a wide grin. Don't forget to avoid Sister on your way out." "Aye, I reckon I'd better be off." The man turned for the door. Later on when we had finished the list of appointments and were clearing up, I asked the Houseman if there was anyone called Harry Rags on the staff. He gave me a funny look and dissolved into laughter. He never did tell me why.

The psychiatric clinic was held every Thursday and it was the main clinic in an uneventful day. Here were seen the patients who were not deranged enough to be admitted to a psychiatric hospital, but who had aberrations that required expert treatment. A few of these patients looked distinctly odd, but the greater majority were just ordinary people. Ordinary, that is, until one sat in the consulting room and listened to their conversation. If we were not busy Sister would allow the student nurses to spend a morning in the consulting room to gain experience in psychiatric problems. These mornings were extremely enlightening. The Psychiatrist would explain each case history and the best method of treatment before the next patient was called in.

One patient in particular I remember. He suffered from delusions, he believed himself to be General Kitchener. This sounds like a classic case. There have been many cartoons drawn about patients sitting outside a psychiatrists waiting room in the attitude of Napoleon. Few people realise that such delusions actually do occur. How they begin is a mystery best left to the psychiatrist and the patient. This man, Mr Moon, was convinced that he was General Kitchener. He could tell anyone who asked all about Kitcheners history and campaigns. As he was talking one suddenly realised that he actually believed it himself. It was no act put on for anyone's benefit. As far as Mr Moon was concerned, he *was* General Kitchener.

The ante natal clinic was our busiest morning clinic. Every Wednesday we would be rushed off our feet from 7.30am until 12 mid day. There were mothers to weigh, urines to test, case histories to be taken and all this with an ear on the buzzer to send in the next patient. In the middle of all this one of the mothers came up to me. "I'm a bit worried, nurse, I'm getting contractions and the baby isn't due for another four weeks." I settled the mother on a sofa in the rest room, and reassured her by telling her that false labour was by no means uncommon. She settled down and I went on with the clinic. After about half an hour I popped back to see how she was getting on. I found her sitting in a wet uncomfortable heap. "My waters have just broken nurse," she informed me. Having no experience of midwifery whatsoever, I wasn't even sure what she meant. I gave her clean linen and went in search of Sister. "Oh, good," said Nettie, "I haven't had the chance of a delivery in five years." When we got to the rest room Mrs Morris burst out, "I want to push, Sister." "Just hang on a minute dear, while I get organised." Nettie said breezily, and told me to go and tell the doctor what was happening. "Oh yes," he said, "Well I'll leave it in Sister's capable hands, she'll call me if she needs me," and with that, he buzzed for the next patient. The delay had caused a backlog of patients and upset my order of things considerably. By the time I had got my clinic sorted out Nettie was coming out of the rest room beaming all over her face. "It's a girl, a little redhead," she said. She sent Staff Nurse off to arrange for an ambulance to the maternity hospital, and got Nurse Walters to clean up the rest room. Mrs Morris was one of those fortunate mothers who experience no pain with their contractions, and whose babies come quickly into the world. Debbie, the baby, had taken just one hour from the time I settled Mrs Morris into the rest room.

It is common knowledge that nurses in some hospitals are required to wear black stockings. In most hospitals the wearing of jewellery on duty is forbidden. Make up is even taboo in other hospitals, but the most unusual restriction I have encountered is being forbidden to wear frilly nylon or silk underwear. An unusual request only until the reason is given. In modern operating theatres there is a great deal of electronic equipment, and also highly inflammable liquid gases. The friction of nylon against the nurses body generates static electricity and if a tiny spark were thus formed near an anaesthetic machine containing ether or some other liquid, an explosion could occur. There was a lot of good natured teasing of the nurses after a notice went up in theatre forbidding silk and nylon underwear. The Consultant would stroll in on operating day. "Good morning, Sister, and what are your nurses wearing today?" he would enquire. "Nothing to raise a blush," Sister would reply if she thought we were out of hearing distance. Betty Frampton, one of the nurses on theatre at the same time as me always wore very pretty underwear. She would often be heard to remark that the nurses uniforms were so plain and ordinary that she felt she had to wear something pretty underneath to compensate for this. When the notice went up advising girls to wear cotton undies while in theatre, Betty was most indignant. "Well," she said. "If it must be cotton, let's see if I can glamorise it." I must confess, I wondered how on earth she could glamorise plain cotton. I wasn't left wondering for long. The next morning as I walked into Theatre changing room a brilliant flash of colour hit me. Betty had dyed all her white cotton underwear a bright scarlet and trimmed it with lace. We awarded her first prize for ingenuity. The funniest part was yet to come. Through constant boiling and wear some of the white theatre dresses go worn and thin. Betty had picked one of these old ones. It was so worn it was almost transparent, and her scarlet bra and briefs were visible to everyone in Theatre.

There was always a big scuffle to get at the Theatre overshoes. There were six pairs of shoes and seven nurses on theatre. Whoever was last in the queue would spend the morning cleaning in the ante room and sorting out the linen cupboard because they couldn't go into Theatre in ordinary shoes. This went on for about four months, then Sue Lane, one of our more militant nurses, decided to go to Sister and demand more Theatre shoes. One of the reasons student nurses seldom get anything new is that they are discouraged from demanding anything by the amount of red tape involved. Sue demanded shoes from Sister, Sister put the demand through to Senior Sister, Senior Sister asked Assistant Matron, Matron signed the demand and sent it to the stores. The stores clerk handed it to the stores superintendent, who sent a man to inspect the old shoes in Theatre. The outcome was that a month later, when Sue had finished her time on Theatre, we received seven new pairs of shoes. All size sixes, two without laces.

While I was on Theatre the hospital management committee had an enquiry into the efficiency of the domestic staff. One of the cleaners had been clocking on in the mornings, going out for the day and coming back in time to clock out. This had been going on for several months and eventually he was found out. The hospital management committee called a meeting to investigate the case. They evidently decided that, as this had been going on undetected for some months at the expense of the hospital, an enquiry was needed to find out how he could have got away with it for so long. They really went to town. A team of time and motion study experts were called in. For weeks they walked around behind the cleaners, porters and orderlies with notebooks and pencils at the ready. The cleaners were quite annoyed, they considered this a slur on their efficiency. In the end, stirred up by Joe, one of the porters, they decided to send a petition to the domestic supervisor. We never knew the outcome of this petition. The bowler hatted men were in the hospital for another couple of weeks. Eventually a whole new set of procedures was worked out and the cleaners were given a typewritten sheet of paper each with new methods of work on them. This enquiry was a good thing from the point of view of the nurses because we were relieved of some of the non nursing duties that we had been doing as part of our routine.

Joe, the militant porter on Theatre had been in the Army Medical Core for twelve years. He was a hardened old soldier. He had travelled all over the world and had seen service on the front line in France. Sometimes when we weren't busy in Theatre he would entertain us with tales of his travels and experiences in wartime France. One story in particular we found amusing. Tension among the troops waiting to go into action was high and it happened that one or two of the young soldiers would crack under the strain. Nights spent in muddy trenches, and interminable hours just waiting for the enemy to attack proved too much for some of the boys. There was one private, just a boy of nineteen or so, who suddenly started acting strangely. He developed a vacant expression and spent all his time looking for a little piece of white paper. At roll call he would be on parade, and suddenly he would stoop down and start searching around the floor. On Church Parade he would start looking under the seats, in the billet he would lift up the mattress and move the mats about five or six times a day. When asked about it, all he would say was, "I'm looking for a little piece of paper." Eventually, this came to the notice of the medical officer, and from there to the psychiatrist. The outcome was that he was declared mentally unsound and discharged from the service. The day before he was shipped home, he came into Joe's office and threw down his discharge note on the desk. "I've found it, mate," he said to Joe. "There's my piece of paper, my ticket to Blighty." It sounded far fetched to us, but Joe swore it was the truth.

Another of Joe's improbable stories was about one of the servicemen's wives. Every time her husband was put on guard duty she would phone the Medical Centre at about one o clock in the morning calling the Medical Officer out for some emergency or other. One night the phone rang, it was this woman in a highly agitated state. "Send the doctor, quick, Michael's swallowed some sleeping tablets." The officer rushed to the house, only to find the little boy quietly asleep, breathing naturally. "Are you quite sure Michael swallowed some pills," he asked. She looked sheepish. "Well, no he didn't really doctor but it's so lonely here when my husband is on guard that I had to talk to somebody."

Joe would tell us about the WRAC girl who reported to sick quarters one morning. On asking her what the problem was, she said, "I've got a touch of pregnancy." Her diagnosis proved correct, and she was discharged.

There are four hospitals in the city where I trained and they take it in turns to receive the weekend casualties. Theatre is quiet on a weekend usually and the nurses fill in time by folding swabs, sorting out linen, sterilising gloves and any other odd jobs. When our hospital is, 'on take,' a weekend on theatre can be hectic. Any road accidents needing immediate surgery are sent to us. Emergency appendectomies, haemorrhages, industrial accidents and anything else needing immediate operation. We had to be prepared for anything. There was always a basic trolley laid up, the sterilisers were kept boiling and the Theatre in readiness. Sometimes a weekend went by with no emergencies at all, but other times we had maybe six or seven cases in an evening. One Saturday night I had been on duty for four hours and the phone had been silent. I thought I would snatch a cat nap on the Theatre table. I settled down with a trolley cover over me, and was soon asleep. I awoke with a start to find the Theatre lights full on and a figure in a mask and gown standing over me with a massive pair of forceps. One of the Housemen, Jim Matheson, had come up to Theatre to scrounge a cup of coffee. Seeing no one about, he had gone in search of somebody and had seen me asleep through the porthole window in the Theatre door. After that I made sure that if I slept on duty, it was somewhere unobtrusive. When I had recovered enough to make the coffee there was no time to drink it. The phone rang, could we take an emergency intestinal obstruction? Jim did this in a record time of twenty minutes. I was just clearing up and boiling up some more instruments when it rang again. "Could we do a gastroscopy?" A little boy had swallowed a halfpenny. We cleared this away and gave the boy back his halfpenny. Ten minutes break before another phone call. A road accident. A man with a depressed fracture of the skull and signs of cerebral oedema. Jim didn't feel he could tackle this one without help so he called out the Chief. More instruments rooted out and boiled up, blood transfusions ordered in case they were needed. Equipment for hypothermia prepared and a technician aroused to deal with it. The patient was wheeled in. Skin cold and clammy, pulse rapid and weak, back arched showing cerebral irritation. As I was senior nurse on Theatre at the time, it fell to me to scrub up for the craniotomy. I was petrified. I had seen brain surgery on a film in the lecture hall, but that was the full extent of my knowledge. There was no alternative, though, and I had to slap the instruments into the Chief's waiting palm with as much efficiency as if I knew what it was all about. Fortunately, however, surgery is fairly straightforward and there are certain basic instruments for all procedures. Jim sensed my predicament, and gave me a nod if I picked up the right one, and a frown if I didn't. The Chief removed a section of bone and probed about until he found a small clot of blood. This he removed and cauterised the tiny blood vessel. Replacing the bone, he stitched up the flap of skin to the scalp and the operation was finished. The patient made an excellent recovery. Half an hour went by after we had cleared up theatre and we settled down to our belated cup of coffee. Surely that's the last emergency, but no, the phone rings again. "Could we do an appendectomy?" Theatre was prepared again. For the fourth time that night I scrubbed up. The patient was a young girl of fourteen or so. Obviously in poor condition. It was found that the appendix had perforated. If she had been an hour later her chances of survival would have been reduced by half. Jim made the incision, a small neat one about two inches in length, and evil smelling pus gushed out. We exchanged glances. This would be more than a straightforward appendectomy. I signalled the assistant nurse to put another set of instruments in to boil and lay up another trolley. In cases of a perforated appendix the contents of the abscess are spread over the intestine and there is a big job of mopping and cleaning up the pus to be done before the Surgeon can proceed to remove the offending organ. Two separate trolleys of instruments are used because of the danger of spreading infection. Jim prided himself on his appendectomies, he maintained that his were the smallest and neatest scars in the hospital especially on young ladies, who tended to be scar conscious. This one was to prove an exception. The two inch scar had to be lengthened for him to get in and clean up the mess. A five inch scar resulted although it was clean cut and healed well. The only concession Jim could make was to do the incision below the bikini line. That proved to be the last case in an eventful night. It was dawn by the time we had got everything organised, and I crawled off duty to sink into bed.

The swabs used in surgical operations are squares of gauze folded and packed into bundles of twenty five. They have an Xray opaque blue line down the centre. Great care is taken to count the swabs during an operation because of the danger of leaving one inside the patient. There is a board on Theatre wall where the number of swabs is recorded before the operation. Halfway through the operation they are counted again, and before the Surgeon closes the incision. If the number of swabs does not correspond with the number on the board the surgeon will not close up. A search is made until the missing swab is found. Melanie Roberts, one of the new nurses on Theatre, was unaware of the importance of the swab count. Halfway through one of the operations she took a dirty trolley out of Theatre to clean it. She threw away five dirty swabs. When the final count was called these five swabs could not be accounted for. Everyone was alerted and a thorough search began. The Surgeon looked inside the patient, Sister looked in all the trolleys, and the nurses looked all around the floor. Suddenly it occurred to Sister that Melanie might not know about the swab count. She went into the sluice in search of her, "Yes," Melanie said, she had cleared the trolley. "Yes," there were swabs on it. "How many?" "Oh, about five." Poor Melanie, she wondered why Sister was rolling her eyes and sighing. Anyway, the swabs were accounted for and the Surgeon was free to close the incision.

There are racks in Theatre for dirty swabs. There are five rows of five prongs on the racks and the swabs are hung up as soon as they are used. This is so that anyone can see at a glance the number used. After some of the longer operations, hole in the heart surgery, for instance, many bundles of swabs are used and all the racks in theatre have to be brought into play. After about four or five hours the Theatre begins to look like a Communist laundry, rows and rows of red swabs.

Chapter 9

A question often asked by old people on admission to hospital is, "How am I going to pay for all this, nurse?" Older people are sometimes unaware that the National Health Service exists. This is often the reason why an old person delays going to the doctor. They are afraid that his fees will take all their savings. Mr Rawlings was a nice old man of seventy five. He was admitted via casualty with a bleeding duodenal ulcer. He was in a very poor state of health. The milkman had called and found him sitting on the stairs, too weak to get up. When Jim Davies came to examine him he asked why he hadn't been to the doctor before. The symptoms must have been troubling him for months. "Well, Doc, on my bit of pension I couldn't go running up no doctors bills," he said. Jim was amazed. This was the first time he had come up against the fact that people can pay contributions without realising what they are for. Jim explained to Mr Rawlings that he had been paying National Health contributions for years, and that he was entitled to all the hospital and doctor's care he was receiving. Another similar case was Mrs Wentworth. She, too, was admitted via Casualty after having collapsed in the street. A mild heart attack was diagnosed and she was treated accordingly. She made a good recovery as far as outward signs and symptoms were concerned, but the Doctors and Sister felt that there was something holding her back. She slept badly and seemed pre occupied most of the time. The almoner came to have a few talks with her and to find out if anything was bothering her. She had a pleasant little cottage and a daughter living not too far away who would come in and look after her. Outwardly everything seemed fine, but as the time drew near for her to be discharged she became visibly worried. We wondered at first if she was becoming hospitalised. This is the term nurses use for patients who are so happy and comfortable in hospital that they are reluctant to go home and fend for themselves. Sister didn't seem to think this was the case, and she had more experience in these matters than us. At last the day came for her to be sent home. I was helping her to pack her belongings when she suddenly caught hold of my arm and started to cry. I pulled the screens around and sat down by her bed to have a little talk and find out what was upsetting her. It appeared that all the time she had been in hospital she had been worrying about how she was going to pay the bill. She was under the impression that she would receive a bill as she went out of the door, and she had no savings to meet it. Old people are often fiercely proud, and she hadn't mentioned it to anyone because she had the old people's dread of, 'living on the parish,' as she put it. I was happy to be able to reassure her.

Mrs Gleeson was another old lady who thought she would receive a bill from the hospital. This time she wasn't worried about where the money was coming from as she had ample funds to meet any expenses. She was admitted suffering from a fractured femur, the result of a fall. On the morning after her admission she called me to the bedside. "Nurse, I want you to do something for me," she whispered. "Ere's the key to my house. I want you to go there and get a packet from the cupboard under the stairs, It's very important, love." When I asked what was in the packet she said darkly. "Never 'ee mind, love, first go and get it, see, I needs it." I didn't say yes at once, I could imagine myself being arrested for burglary and all sorts of things. She seemed genuinely upset when I hesitated, and so I decided to take a chance and go. She lived some miles out of town in a dingy little side street. Fitting the key into the lock, I went in. There was a musty smell to the place but it appeared to have been well looked after. I opened the windows, found a duster and tidied up a little. There was a brown paper parcel in the cupboard under the stairs, just as she had said. It was extremely light, although it was large. I gave it to Mrs Gleeson the next morning when I went on duty. "Ah," she said thankfully. "I'm glad you found it, pull the screens around, would you, love." We were quite busy on the ward and Sister was on the warpath, so I said I would come back later when we were quiet. "Now." she said and the note of command in her voice so surprised me that I obeyed automatically. "Now that Doctor said I would likely be in here some six weeks," she began, "and I'd be running up a bit of a bill, I expect." Before I could break in and tell her otherwise, she continued. "Now this 'ere is a bit I've been saving up for my children when I go, but there aint one of 'em as deserves it. I want you to take it. After the Doctor's bills have been settled, share the rest out between you girls, you deserve it. I couldn't do a dirty old job like you do for all the money in the world." She had opened the parcel while she was talking and there on the bed, and spilling on to the floor were piles and piles of grubby pound notes. I was terrified now in case Sister should burst in through the screens and see me with all that money. She would be sure to think that I was encouraging the old lady to give it away. Hastily, I tried to explain that there were no hospital bills, and the nurses didn't accept money anyway. She didn't seem to understand at all, and was in the middle of giving me a lecture about being too proud to accept a gift, when Sister actually did burst in. Far from being annoyed, she took in the situation at a glance. Apparently she had come up against this sort of thing before. She sent me away to attend to the dressings and remained behind the screens with old Mrs Gleeson. What went on I never found out, but Mrs Gleeson proudly announced a few days later that she had opened a bank account and was getting interest on her money. She had insisted, however, that the nurses should have something, and so Sister allowed her to send for a large bottle of hand cream, which was placed in the sluice. A practical present in a practical place.

Coming on duty next evening I found Mrs Gleeson sitting up in bed in a magnificent nightie. It was very fine lawn, with hand made lace down the front. It was beautifully made and truly remarkable for its air of Victorian craftsmanship. I remarked on the gossamer fineness of the lace. "Ah yes," she began. "They don't make lace like this nowadays. Sixty years old, this nightie is. I made it when I was a young girl of eighteen, first married. It's been wrapped up in tissue paper in the attic. I've been keeping it to be buried in, but I thought I may as well wear it. It'll rot and mould 'afore I die," she cackled. "Get me up and walking and I'll live to be a hundred yet." She probably will, too.

Many diseases are named after the person that described them or the part of the country where they are most prevalent. 'Derbyshire neck,' is an example. It describes the simple goitre that is prevalent in Derbyshire, also in Switzerland and certain parts of America. It had something to do with a lack of iodine in the water. It is rarely seen these days as Iodine is usually added to water. The other type of goitre is named after the man who first described it. Graves disease is named after the surgeon Robert Graves. The main difference between Graves disease and the so called, 'Derbyshire neck,' is that the former is toxic and has distressing side effects. It is caused by over activity of the thyroid gland.

Ann Randall, a senior nurse on Ely Ward was a typical thyroid type. She had bulging brown eyes, a slight swelling in her neck and a bustling, flapping manner. She was always irritable. If anyone hinted in her hearing that she was thyrotoxic she would deny it hotly. It was never proved, of course, but her symptoms were more classic than many of the patients that she nursed.

Christmas disease is a type of haemophilia. It was described in 1952 by a team of doctors led by Dr Biggs, a woman. The little boy in whom the disease was discovered was named Christmas, and the factor in the blood, the lack of which causes bleeding is called the Christmas factor. Reynauds disease in a mild form is quite common. Only severe cases are referred to the hospital It is characterised by a spasm of the blood vessels to the fingers and sometimes the toes on contact with the cold. The blood supply is diminished and the fingers go deadly white. In severe cases gangrene may develop. Mrs Norris was a patient on Ely ward with Reynauds disease. She claimed to be able to tell if the weather was cold simply by putting her hands out of the bedclothes in the morning. If they turned white the weather was cold. Whenever we wanted an unofficial weather forecast we consulted Mrs Norris.

Hodgkins disease is another condition named after the man who first described it. Thomas

Hodgkin was a pathologist at Guys in the early 19th century. He was known to be eccentric, and showed complete disregard for money, often not bothering to collect his fees from patients who could well afford them. He was a Quaker and a graduate of Edinburgh University. In his later years he gave up the medical world to travel, and died of dysentery in the Far East in 1866. He wrote a paper describing the clinical features of Hodgkins disease. It had no name then, but was just a collection of symptoms consisting of enlargement of the lymph glands throughout the body, giving rise to pressure symptoms within the abdomen and chest.

Thomas Addison was another Guy's physician, one of only a few who gave their name to two diseases. He, too was a graduate of Edinburgh University and a contemporary of James Bright. Together they wrote 'Elements of practical medicine' which was published in 1839. Addisons disease is a rare condition characterised by wasting of the supra renal glands. It may be tuberculous in origin. The patient's skin is mottled and of a coppery colour owing to pigmentation. The other disease, the discovery of which was attributed to Addison was Addisons anaemia. Pernicious anaemia was another name for it. In the far off days before modern drugs were heard of, this disease was always fatal, hence the name pernicious anaemia. It is curable with modern techniques, but the name still sticks.

James Paget 1814-1889, was a surgeon at St Bartholomews Hospital. He was physician to Queen Victoria and other royal personages. He was one of seventeen children and began work as an apprentice to a Yarmouth apothecary at an early age. During Paget's time at Barts the first women doctors were trained. The first woman doctor on the roll, Elizabeth Blackwell MD, had been a student of his. He was not enthusiastic, but he tolerated women in the profession. Paget, like Addison, described two diseases. Pagets disease of bone, or osteitis deformans, a condition where there is gross deformity of the long bones due to softening, and changes in the shape of the head, again due to softening of the bones. The patients are usually elderly and loss of height is noticeable. There is no recognised treatment. The other is Pagets disease of the nipple. A dry eczematous rash appears round the nipple in elderly women. It does not respond to treatment, gradually it erodes the nipple and in later stages a carcinomatous growth is discovered. Treatment is by removal of the breast as soon as the eczematous rash has been diagnosed definitely as Pagets disease. There is a high recovery rate after this operation.

William Stokes gave his name to two clinical conditions, not in themselves diseases. He studied medicine at Dublin, Glasgow and Edinburgh. He was greatly interested in diseases of the chest and heart. Stokes Adams syndrome is the name given to a particular type of heart block. A condition where the auricles contract at a different rate from, and independently of, the ventricle of the heart. One of the main features is an extremely low pulse rate and sometimes momentary loss of consciousness. This comes in attacks and may persist over a number of years. The first account of these syndromes was described by Adams, a friend and colleague of Stokes in 1827.

The second condition Stokes described was the particular kind of breathing observed in seriously ill and dying patients. Cheyne Stokes respirations. John Cheyne, in 1818 noticed this type of respiration in one of his patient with heart failure. Stokes described more cases. Cheyne-Stokes respirations are well known to most nurses. They are unmistakable. The patient's breathing is quiet, almost undetectable at first. It gradually gets louder and deeper, reaching a peak, and dies down again. When there is a long silence and the patient doesn't breathe at all for about a quarter of a minute, then the process starts all over again. Any nurse will tell you of the patient she has specialled all night and who has been, 'Cheyne-Stoking.' There are no other noises in the ward and she sits by the bedside of this patient, often an old man who has suffered a stroke, or maybe a young victim of a motorbike accident. His breathing reaches its peak in a long, shuddering gasp, then recedes gradually until the pause comes. The nurse waits, and waits. Just when she thinks he can't possibly breathe again, there it comes, a faint, barely perceptible intake of breath mounting up to another climax. This breathing has a strangely hypnotic effect on the nurse. She feels compelled to listen to it because, subconsciously, she realises that after one of the pauses he may not start breathing again.

At the beginning of the third year we received a few pep talks from the Sister Tutor. "You are responsible young ladies now, you have been almost prepared for State Registration. Don't let the training school down," etc. In fact the thing that would have worried most of us, had we failed was the fact that we would have lost the examination fees. Most nurses are only quick in defence of their training school if someone from a different hospital criticises it. Then we defend it with all the arguments and knowledge at our disposal. Ordinarily, it can go hang!

Another big issue in the final year is whether the nurse will live outside the hospital or stay in the nurses home. I chose to live out, protesting that I couldn't stand hospital meals a minute longer. Then began the hunt for a place to live. Every day Joyce Thomson and I would eagerly scan the evening paper, pencil in hand, looking for flats and rooms. Every day as soon as duty was over we would rush out to see whatever was available. We looked at practically every flat within a six mile radius. We saw luxury flats with heavy velvet curtains (no children or pets allowed). Basement flats, weirdly decorated and damp. Blocks of one room bedsits at exorbitant prices, built purely for profit without much concern for comfort. Everything we saw was either too expensive or downright slummy. After about three weeks of solid searching we were thinking of remaining in the nurses home and giving up the search. One evening I was at a coffee bar with the girls when we ran into a girl who had started training with us, but who had left to take up modelling. That hadn't lasted either, and now she was a typist. In the course of our conversation she mentioned that she was in a flat big enough for four, but they had to move out because there were only two of them and they couldn't afford the rent. This was just the opportunity we needed so I asked if they would stay on if they could find another two to share expenses. She jumped at the chance and so, with the help of her boy friend's ancient Mercedes, we moved in the following week. It was a beautiful flat, large and airy with a panoramic view at the front and a brick wall at the back. Now began the task of keeping house for ourselves. Babs and Evelyn, the two typists we shared with decided that, as we worked shifts and they worked office hours, we would keep our groceries separate. There were two big food cupboards, so, having a look at what they had in theirs we made a list and rushed off to the grocery shop. (No supermarkets in the 1960's). Neither of us had any experience of shopping for food. We went wild. Joyce had a liking for spicy food, Indian curries and hot pickles. I was not so adventurous, I have since developed a taste for them. Not the way Joyce used to cook them, though. The Grocery shop was like a great glistening web, and we were two unsuspecting flies. We came out so loaded down that we had to call a taxi to take us home - an unheard of luxury. The novelty of doing our own cooking soon wore off and we sneaked back to the hospital dining room for illicit meals more and more often.

Joyce was being courted by a commercial traveller at the time, and sometimes he would stay the night on the sofa in the living room. (before the days of co-habitation). Evelyn, too had a boyfriend who lived thirty miles away and rode an unreliable motor bike, so whenever it broke down he would spend the night in the living room, too. Returning one weekend from a trip to Wales, I arrived at the flat at about midnight. Switching on the light I saw what seemed to be a mass of bodies sprawled in various positions all over the living room floor. There was Joyce's Bill, there was Evelyn's John, smelling of motor oil and there was a new face, someone I had never seen before. I quickly switched the light off and crept through to the bedroom. There was someone in my bed! This was the last straw, men in the living room I didn't mind, but a girl in my bed, when I had travelled all the way from Wales on a late train filled with soldiers and airmen. This was the limit. While I was standing there wondering where I was going to sleep, Babs turned over and said sleepily "Oh heck, what are you doing home." What a greeting! They hadn't been expecting me for another day and the girl in my bed was Babs's sister. The new boy in the living room was her boyfriend. Eventually Babs and I dragged a mattress to a corner of the floor, and there I slept with only a few cockroaches for company. I was glad to get up for work at 5am. The mattress had been so uncomfortable. By way of a contrast, when I came home that afternoon, the birds had flown. The flat was quite empty.

Our flat was one of four, a basement flat and three storeys. The milkman would leave milk for all the flats on the front doorstep. Needless to say, this resulted in occasional bouts of confusion. We managed fairly well though, working on the principle that if we were a pint short one day, we had had a pint over the day before. There was an unspoken agreement among the occupants that it was first come, first served, and we didn't quibble about the odd pint of milk. That is, until the policeman and his wife moved in to the first floor flat.

They were obviously newlyweds, Evelyn had seen him carry her across the threshold a few weeks previously. We decided to leave them alone and made no attempt to communicate with them more than the customary 'good morning'. One day when I was alone in the flat there was a knock at the door. It was the policeman, unshaven, in a dressing gown. "You haven't taken an extra pint of milk by mistake, have you?" I assured him that we had not, and heard him trudging up the other flight of stairs. This was the beginning of the end as far as our unspoken agreement about milk went. After that, every time anyone took an extra pint, it turned out to be the policeman's. After three or four missing pints he got quite irate and would wait just inside the door of the flat to see how many pints everyone had, and he even questioned the milkman to see how many pints we all paid for. In the end we would steal in quietly and, looking left and right we would snatch up our own pint of milk that we had paid for, from the doorstep and scuttle upstairs with it, waiting for a shout of, 'stop thief,' from the flat below.

Evelyn was an ardent pop fan, she had a little radio and wherever she went the radio was sure to go. We were sitting one afternoon listening to the radio. We had decided to have a relaxing day, Evelyn was drying her hair and the other two were lounging around in house coats when a knock sounded at the door. I was the most respectable at that moment so I answered it. On the threshold was a civil servant type of man, pin stripes and bowler. "Do you own a radio?" he enquired. Without stopping to think, I said yes. "Is it licensed?" the next question brought me up with a start. Was it licensed? I was fairly sure it wasn't, knowing Evelyn. "Could I speak to the owner of the radio, please?" the little man said. Gratefully I disappeared in to the living room to get her. "I can't answer the door with my hair like this." she wailed. "Well, what am I to do?" I demanded, "ask him in?" this was greeted by a chorus of protest from Babs and Joyce, both unsuitably dressed to receive visitors. I went back to the door. "The owner of the radio can't come because her hair is all wet," I began lamely. "Well will you ask her if her set is licensed?" he said pleasantly. I shouted through to Evelyn who replied after a noticeable pause, "Of course it is." "May I see the license, please," he demanded. I went through to fetch it and found Evelyn in a panic. "It's not licensed," she blurted out. Here my patience ended. "Go and tell him yourself." I said, pushing her to the front door, curlers and all. The outcome of this was that Evelyn had to buy a license for the radio and pay a fine for making a false declaration. "Why on earth didn't you tell him we had no radio?" she demanded when he had gone. "What? With 'pick of the pops' blaring out at full volume?" I replied.

Our flat was half an hours walk from the hospital so we usually caught a bus. The early morning rush hour was a bad time for getting to work. Joyce and I invariably left it until the last minute to catch a bus, so if the bus was full up we had to walk. There is a considerable difference between a ten minute bus ride and a thirty minute walk, so if the bus was full we were usually late on duty. This was all right if we happened to know the Staff Nurse who signed the student nurses in, but if it was a new one or a nasty one, we would marked down as late. Three late marks in a week and we went before Matron. A long series of late marks, and we lost the chance to live out. There were any number of dodges to avoid a late mark. One was to telephone a friend and ask her to book you in. This was OK if the Sister wasn't on duty in the morning. If she was, and you were late she would phone Matron's office and report you absent. Then, of course, Matron would want to know who had booked you in. Alternatively you could phone the Staff Nurse and tell her you were on your way. Note: mobile phones hadn't been invented then, so finding a phone box would delay you further. If she was a good sort you wouldn't get a late mark. The first time I was late, I made the mistake of phoning Matron's office and telling them I was walking in to work. "Get a taxi, nurse," was the curt command. "The hospital does not pay you to be late for work." I had four shillings until the end of the month. It all had to go on a taxi. After that, if I was late and couldn't wangle the book, I would just take my time and arrive when I could, saying nothing and hoping nobody had noticed.

In between regular boy friends Babs would run wild and go to all the jazz clubs and dances advertised. This would continue for about three weeks then she would meet someone special at one of the dances and embark on another six weeks of steady dates. Unfortunately she never bothered to tell the man of the moment that it was all over, she just failed to turn up one evening, leaving a message to say that she had gone to the jazz club instead. Consequently there were always a few of Bab's ex boy friends ringing the doorbell. One such persistent suitor was Mike. He had a special ring on the doorbell, three short peals, so that we always knew who it was. One evening we were tactfully preparing to go out and leave Babs in the flat with Bob, her latest conquest, when the doorbell rang. Three short peals. We all looked at each other. Babs looked horror stricken. Mutely her eyes appealed to one of us to answer the bell. Mike had become an old friend, and if we answered the door he would expect to be let in. He wasn't very quick on the uptake, either, and if he saw Bob in the flat it probably would not occur to him that he was with

Babs. While we were hesitating Bob jumped up. "I'll go," he said and bounded to the door before anyone could stop him. We sat there holding our breath, waiting for the sounds of a fight or at the very least, raised voices. Within minutes Bob returned looking quite unperturbed. "Who was it?" I asked, trying to sound casual. "Only somebody for a Miss Hampton," he replied. "I don't know anyone of that name, do you? Bob, being a very new boyfriend hadn't had time to learn Babs surname yet. Doubtless, he would find out.

Nurses uniforms have long been a subject for heated discussion. When short skirts became fashionable we signed a petition demanding at least five inches off our uniform dresses and aprons and sent it to matron's office. There was no direct reply, but a notice was posted up in the nurses dining room. "With the rapidly changing fashions of today, we at Matron's office are not prepared to instruct the dressmakers to shorten uniform dresses. If we did this, we would be bombarded with requests to lengthen them within six months. The purpose of uniform is uniformity, and not to dress the junior members of the profession as they wish." This was an unusual break with tradition, Matron's office did not usually give reasons for it's actions. Although indignant, we were quite amused at their reasoning. When short skirts had been in fashion another year we again petitioned the office for shorter uniforms, referring to the date in their last reply. We pointed out that skirts were being worn even shorter, with no foreseeable return to mid calf length. There was a notice on the board the following day. 'Would all student nurses report to the sewing room between 9 and 11am with their dresses ready for alteration'. We were jubilant. One little victory against authority. Heartened by this we petitioned the office more and more over little things that hitherto had not bothered us unduly. After months of this Matron made it known that petitions from the student nurses would no longer be accepted. We were to elect a spokesman for each set, who would be free to see Matron on a set day and state any grievances. Any student nurses, even the boldest, when confronted by Matron in all her majesty, is hesitant to speak freely so this idea was not held in much regard by the nurses. Matron probably realised this when she planned it. One of the earliest references to nurses uniforms can be found in the letters of Florence Nightingale. In it she refers to, 'the remarkable sight afforded to patients when the nurse bends to attend to the needs of some sick soldier at Scutari, wearing a crinoline.' Florence Nightingale died in 1910, but confrontations between students and Matron's office over uniform are still much in evidence.

Many of the diseases prevalent in Florence Nightingale's time are now practically non existent but other, seemingly newer diseases have arisen to take their place. Bubonic plague is almost unheard of in Britain these days. In the seventeenth century there was the great epidemic that carried away more than half of the population of London, and it was seen sporadically until the early part of the twentieth century. There is virtually no bubonic plague these days, but more subtle psychological conditions seem to replace it.

The first case of appendicitis was described in 1812. Nowadays it is common, but rarely fatal. Diphtheria was a killer until fairly recent times.

Now, with facilities for immunisation for all babies, it is rarely seen. Until the discovery of penicillin in recent years, pneumonia was a dreaded disease, especially in the British climate. Now it has been conquered. The task of the nurse now, compared with twenty years ago is vastly different or, shall we say, the practical bedside nursing care is basically the same. To attend to the patient's needs and to ensure his comfort. It is the manner of ensuring his comfort that has changed. Twenty years ago a case of pneumonia for example, would have been nursed in bed, with all the nursing care that entails. Someone had to sit at the bedside to watch for the Crisis. Cool sponges to reduce the temperature, and weeks in bed convalescing to make up the energy used in overcoming the disease. Nowadays a case of pneumonia is still nursed in bed. That is the only similarity. With the advent of penicillin the 'pneumonia crisis' went out. The drug gently and quietly goes to work in the body breaking down the barriers of the disease, keeping the temperature down and allowing the patient to conserve his own energy to get well. If there is respiratory distress there are piped supplies of oxygen to the larger hospitals, and cylinders to the smaller ones. There is the oxygen tent as well to relieve the patients breathing. The convalescent period is much shorter because the patient, on the whole, is much fitter than he would have been if his body's defences had to fight the pneumonia bacillus alone.

The approach to marriage and childbearing has changed tremendously in the last few decades. Thirty years ago it was rare to have a family of less than four, indeed, fourteen and sixteen children in a family were by no means unusual. The attitude to childbirth, too has changed. Far from being a thing referred to in hushed tones behind closed doors, and never discussed in the presence of the father, parent craft classes are held at local clinics, and both parents are encouraged to attend, see films, hear lectures and ask questions freely. Some of the novels written in the latter part of the nineteenth century give horrifying pictures of childbirth and show the awe in which it was held. There were no trained midwives and the village 'old woman' would deliver all the babies. The term, 'old wives tale,' dates from these times. The poor mother, a girl of seventeen or eighteen would be completely ignorant of the process of labour and delivery and her head would be filled with the terrifying tales that the older women seemed to delight in telling. Young mothers are more fortunate now. They are encouraged to attend ante natal clinics where a careful history is taken. They are shown films of actual delivery, and the various stages are explained to them. They know that if they need them, gas and air apparatus and pain killing injections are readily available. The midwife will not hesitate to give them if necessary. If, as sometimes happens, there are complications and a forceps delivery is required, or even a caesarean section, anaesthetics and skilled surgeons are there on call. One can imagine the dread in which childbirth must have been held in the last century. No gas and air, no injections, no anaesthetic and complete ignorance of what was going on. No drugs to control haemorrhage, no antibiotics to treat puerperal fever, or child bed fever as it was then known. With modern methods of contraception, parents have children when they want them, or when they feel they can afford them. Of course, there are exceptions to this rule. In Victorian times the wife's place was at home having children. This was because there was no alternative, she was not trained to any particular job. It was not considered respectable. If she did not marry she was looked upon with scorn or worse, pity. A woman's place was definitely in the home, methods of contraception were primitive, and so the children came, and with each successive pregnancy the health of the mother was undermined. It was quite common for medical students and doctors in those days to go to a confinement straight from an infectious patient or even a post mortem. There was no thought of washing their hands. Germs, as such, were not recognised. The spread of child bed fever was rapid and mostly fatal. In the so called Women's hospitals the midwives would spread the infection throughout the ward on their hand, their shoes, their aprons, and great epidemics of it would kill dozens of mothers at a time. In the fifty years from 1880 to 1930 the death rate was 2000 per annum.

In modern society, with women's emancipation, the pill, nursery schools, antibiotics, relaxation therapy during childbirth and all the hundred and one benefits afforded to us, we are indeed living in a prosperous age. And yet it would seem that the human race always has to keep striving. No sooner is one disease overcome by medicine or surgery than another one makes itself known. The more subtle psychological diseases are prevalent today. Maybe there is not enough to keep people occupied and boredom creeps in and becomes an obsession. Ten years ago a man had to work hard enough to support a growing family. These days wages are higher, the work is lighter, and often the family is smaller. There are countless free hours to hand in which to brood and develop anxiety neuroses. There is the constant threat of nuclear war, if one is of a mind to worry about it. Whatever the reason, our psychiatric hospitals are filled to capacity, mostly with minor ailments which respond to treatment. Nevertheless, a few years ago, a good percentage of patients would not have found their way into hospital, they would have too busy providing for a family to brood.

Chapter 10

Annie, the ward maid on Carter Ward was a wonderful example of motherhood. She had twelve children. All of them were married, working or at school now, and she came part time on the wards. She was extremely proud of her family, as indeed she had every right to be. She was a great source of comfort to the women on the ward. Often they came in for operations, worrying about their families and things at home. Annie was quick to sense these home worries and always had a comforting word ready. "I've reared twelve, love, and had four operations. No harm has ever come to any of them while I've been in here," she would say cheerfully. Annie used to tell us about the time she had her husband as a patient on Miller ward. "Expected me to wait on him hand and foot, he did," she would laugh. "You'd think he was the only patient in the ward the way he carried on. In the end I had to turn around and tell him that, though he was my husband at home, in Miller Ward he was just another number." Her eyes would crinkle up with laughter as she recalled his surprise. Annie cared for nobody, be he consultant or student. She said exactly what she thought with no regard for anyone, yet everybody loved her. She always noticed if any of the nurses missed their coffee break through pressure of work, and had a kettle boiling in the kitchen when the nurse had more time.

One evening I was on duty with Joyce Thomson. We had settled the patients down for the night and Joyce wheeled the trolley with the cups and saucers into the kitchen. I was in the ward tidying up when I heard Joyce shout from the kitchen. To shout in a hospital ward after lights out is almost unheard of, so I rushed in and found Annie lying on the floor, her face blue and gasping for breath. Joyce made her comfortable while I rushed to fetch the oxygen and phone for the Houseman. She had had a coronary thrombosis, and we admitted her to the side ward attached to Carter Ward. She was on the danger list for two or three days. Her family were notified, and all twelve of them came within twenty four hours. I specialled her all the next day, she was semi comatose and her pulse was weak and erratic It was touch and go for the next few days, then gradually she began to gain strength. Within a week she was sitting up and trying to run the ward. After a fortnight she was referred at her own request to the main ward. Although she was not allowed to do anything for herself, she sat, propped up on pillows and watched the temporary ward maid who had come to take her place. Fewer things are so frustrating as watching someone else do your own job, and Annie never gave the poor girl any peace. In the end she went to Sister and requested that Annie be put back in the side ward. Sister had a quiet talk with Annie, and peace reigned once more on the ward.

There was a limit of two visitors at a bed at the same time, so there was some confusion when Annie's twelve children all came to visit her together. They had to take the visiting hour in relays and were allowed ten minutes each with her. The family likeness was remarkable in her children. They all had bright ginger hair, from the eldest, a woman of thirty five, to the youngest, a boy of twelve. Annie's hair was iron grey, and no one would have guessed that it had once been bright ginger, too.

The laws of heredity are strange, I have known a young mother very upset because she had a dark haired baby, and both she and her husband were fair. "What will people think?" she sobbed.

Occasionally we hear of a child with distinctly foreign features being born to two ordinary British parents. They may be Negroid or Oriental, but whatever it is the parents are usually extremely shocked. This phenomena can be often be traced back three or four generations to an African or Asian great great grandparent. Of course, this is very rare, but cases are recorded from time to time.

The question of heredity is complex, and as yet, not fully explained. Why should a baby have curly hair when both the parents have straight hair? Why should a child be left handed when both the parents are right handed? Why should twins run in some families? We know it happens, but as yet we do not know why. When the whole structure of genes is fully understood, maybe we will be able to predict the sex of our unborn child. (Note: this was written before the recent discovery of the Human Genome and all that entails).

Mrs Evans was an orderly on Maternity Ward. She was something of a busybody and liked to find out all she could about the mothers on the ward. Often when Sister would come out of the delivery room, Mrs Evans would want to know all the details of the birth. Confidentiality is sacrosanct, and Sister never gave anything away. Mrs Evans would take the first opportunity to talk to the mother, and there would follow a long discussion about her five confinements. Exactly what the midwife said and did, and how her neighbour had run for the midwife with her last child, and only just got there in time. Although the nursing staff got tired of hearing the same story, the mothers seemed glad of someone to discuss their experiences with. Mrs Evans prided herself on the fact that she was able to tell whether a mother would have a boy or a girl. We all laughed at this idea and Sister was even a bit cross. The strange thing was that she was nearly always right. In twenty five births on the ward, Mrs Evans only made one mistake about the sex of the child. When we questioned her, she would say, "It's simple, you carries a boy in front and a girl behind." I could never fathom out what she meant. The Sister on Maternity ward was married and had been hoping for a baby of her own for about a year. She came on duty one morning and Mrs Evans stopped sweeping up and stared at her for some minutes. Eventually she said, "congratulations, Sister, you'll be leaving us soon, then." Sister was dumbfounded. "What on earth do you mean?" she asked. "There's a baby on the way, that's what I mean," she said. "I only wish there were," Sister laughed. Don't kid me," Mrs Evans said, "I can see it by your face." She said no more, and we forgot the incident. About a fortnight later Sister called Mrs Evans into her office. We don't know what was said, but Mrs Evans came out with an 'I told you so' expression on her face. She spent the rest of the day making dark hints about Sister and the coming baby. Within a few days Sister confirmed the fact and we were happy to congratulate her. We were all agog with curiosity, and bombarded her with questions. How could she tell? Was it second sight? "Of course not," she denied the latter accusation hotly. "You can usually tell by a girl's face when she is pregnant," she said. "I can't describe it, but I know what I mean." It was a good thing she knew what she meant, because nobody else did.

Certain diseases are hereditary. They are passed from generation to generation. One of the most well known is haemophilia. This occurs only in males, and one of the features is a tendency to bleed profusely at the slightest scratch. There was a family of haemophiliacs or bleeders living within a few miles of the hospital. There were four boys and a girl. It was a regular occurrence to have one or even two of the boys in Casualty with cuts and scratches. Normal children take no notice of the occasional scratch, but to a haemophiliac it could mean death if not promptly attended to. Little boys are never content to sit at home. These four insisted on going out and playing all the games that the other boys played. As soon as they thought that no one was watching, they would climb trees and swing out on the branches or get hold of a penknife and start whittling away at a piece of wood. Consequently, the poor mother was always bringing them to Casualty.

There are some families with a particular birth mark appearing on each child. The strawberry mark is quite common, a little cluster of veins bunched together and showing red like a strawberry. This can occur on any part of the body and often occurs in the same place on brothers or sisters.

Mrs Jones was a patient in the Maternity Ward. She was expecting her sixth child. It was a little girl, and the first thing she said was, "Let's see if it's got the trade mark." We wondered if the gas and air had made her drowsy. "Come on, let's have her," she said. Sister handed the baby over, a tiny little bundle with a shock of black hair. Mrs Jones turned her over. There on the left shoulder was a tiny strawberry mark. "Ah," she sighed, "that's all right then." I enquired what this was all about. "Well, I've got five others and they've all got a little strawberry in the same spot, and so has my husband."

Brittle bones run in some families. It is a disease associated with hereditary inability to metabolise calcium in the body. These children usually have one distinctive feature, the whites of their eyes, instead of being white, are china blue. It is quite a rare condition, one case occurring in every five thousand families. There have occasionally been cases where a child has been referred to social services because of several unexplained fractures. This must be a nightmare for the parents, though these days the condition is more widely recognised.

Little Michael Brewer was a mischievous five year old. He had this disease, and so did his three sisters. The Children's Ward was no strange place to them and Sister kept a cot in the corner of the ward for them, so often did they visit us. Michael was admitted with a broken leg, the result of a tumble when playing leapfrog. Two days later the distraught mother brought in Mary, his three year old sister. She had tripped up two steps, put her hands out to support herself, and fractured both wrists. A week later the baby was brought in with a broken arm. She had been chasing a balloon. All three fractures healed well and they were all out within a week.

It is a well known fact that if an expectant mother contracts german measles (rubella) in the first three months of pregnancy it could have an adverse effect on the baby. These days 'german measles parties' are in fashion. If the child gets german measles the mother will send a note to all her friends who have little girls telling them that their child is having a party, and all the mothers who want their daughters to catch the disease should come along. German measles is a mild disease and one attack usually gives immunity for life, so if the girls have it in childhood there will be little danger of catching it in later life. (note, this was written before the rubella vaccine was discovered).

Much publicity has been given to the drug thalidomide, it is a tranquilliser and, if taken in pregnancy can have a devastating effect on the foetus. These days it is very rarely prescribed, and never to expectant mothers. There are, in fact very few things that can harm a baby in the womb. Even a bad fall in pregnancy is not likely to affect the baby. One case is on record where a mother received accidental shotgun wounds to her abdomen during pregnancy. She was admitted to hospital and a caesarean section was performed resulting in a healthy baby. The bullet had gone into the womb and grazed the baby's head, but he made and excellent recovery, and so did the mother, although it took a little longer for her to get well.

While I was living at the nurses home one of the girls reported a prowler in the hospital grounds, this happened fairly often, as previous chapters will tell you. Nobody was actually seen, but several of the girls said that they heard strange noises This started off a craze for burglar alarms. These were many and varied, ranging from a piece of string tied just inside the door a few inches from the floor, to bags of sand rigged up above the door to fall on intruders. Bridget Hallorhan thought up a particularly good one. She filled a cocoa tin with flour and suspended it by a string to the ceiling. As the door opened it would tilt the string and the tin of flour, which was at an angle, would empty its contents over the intruder. Bridget had this contraption rigged up for about two weeks and nothing happened. All the girls knew about it, so if they came to her room they would knock and wait. Bridget herself would open the door slowly, get a stick which she kept out in the corridor, and move the tin enough for her to get inside. Coming off duty one morning, she was dismayed to find that the tin had been tipped. There was flour everywhere. This could only mean one thing. Someone had been in her room. She had given such a startled shout when she discovered the tin of flour that three or four of us had come to see what it was all about. We went up and down the corridor looking for signs of an intruder. There was nothing to see, it had all been swept up by the cleaner.

We almost collided with a breathless figure bounding up the stairs. It was Mary Abbott, one of the Staff nurses. "Hey, Halloran, you're wanted in Matron's office," she shouted. "Whatever for?" began Bridget. "I don't know, but if you'd seen

Home Sister this morning you might be able to guess," she said darkly. When we asked why, Mary said "I saw her with Assistant Matron coming down the corridor today, she was covered in flour." We all stood, open-mouthed. Obviously Home Sister had decided to have one of her inspections. She did this occasionally. It was mere bad luck that Assistant matron was with her. The Home Sister was a good sort, and although Bridget would have received a telling off, Matron would never have got to hear about the incident. The Assistant Matron, however, felt it her duty to report it. Bridget came back from her interview with Matron looking really shaken. "What did she say?" I asked. "Oh, nothing much," she grinned, "just that if I persist in this eccentric behaviour she will have no alternative but to release me from my contract." "Oh yeah! Empty threats again," I smiled. It was nothing new for Matron to threaten a person with dismissal, but the only real reason anyone ever got sent away was if they were expecting a baby, which, in a community of some three hundred girls, occasionally happened.

Towards the end of my three years the sudden realisation dawned that final examinations were only a matter of weeks away. A notice was posted up informing all state finalists that their examination fees were due. This threw us all into a state of panic, not so much the money for the fees, which was bad enough, but knowledge that finals were so near. Before the actual State Finals there were the hospital finals. These were a kind of preliminary to the big exams. If we passed these we earned the hospital badge. The hospital Medical and Surgical staff acted as examiners. It was a good idea really, as it gave us a rough idea of what an examination was like and showed up our weak points before State Finals. There was a practical nursing paper lasting something like three hours, medicine and surgery papers, a practical examination in ward techniques and two oral exams. For the practical exam we had real patients. Three or four of the convalescent patients offered to come up to the teaching unit and lend their services for us. I went in to the practical with Joyce Thomson. We had half an hour of practical work together, then another half hour answering questions on nursing techniques. The first few questions were not too bad. At least they covered questions that we had swotted up, then came a bolt out of the blue. "Lay up a trolley for an antral washout." We looked at each other and I could feel my heart sink. Ear Nose and Throat nursing was my weakest subject. If it had been anything else I could have muddled through somehow, but E N T! This was the end and I knew Joyce felt the same. We went off in search of a trolley and the basic things to put on it. As for the instruments, we just had to guess at them. While I was standing at the instrument cupboard, racking my brains trying to think what to put out, I heard a faint sound from one of the beds. There were three make believe patients in the practical room. The sound came again, a long drawn out sigh in which I could faintly discern the word, 'atomiser.' Catching on quickly and with no feeling of guilt, I put out an atomiser spray for local anaesthetic. Then another faint sigh, 'cannula.' I put out a cannula to puncture the antrum. And so on until I had the trolley laid. The examiner seemed satisfied and we went on with the questions. After the exam I told Joyce about our unknown friend. Obviously an ENT patient. She was disgusted, and all for going to Sister Tutor and telling her the truth. My corrupt nature won in the end, though, and we kept it quiet. We both passed with flying colours too. I blush a little to remember the incident, but not too much.

Next came the oral exam. Fifteen minutes with a Surgical Consultant. This, I thought, would be the biggest ordeal of the lot. The Surgical consultant was a flamboyant character. Everything he said and did was loud. He wore black and white checked suits and an assortment of coloured waistcoats. He could be extremely sarcastic, and many a medical student I have seen reduced to a blushing heap as a result of some cutting remark from him.

I was literally quaking as I went in to the exam room. There were so many questions he could ask, and so few I knew well enough to say much about. "Ah, good morning, nurse," he sounded genial enough, anyway. "Where did you go for your holiday this year?" "Pardon sir," I stammered, unable to believe my ears. "I went to the Costa Brava," he went on, "Beautiful place, lots of swimming, blue seas, blue skies, and golden girls, eh, what." He chuckled. "Ah yes," there was a reminiscent look in his eye. "What it is to be able to sit in a boat and watch the sunset. I'll tell you what, nurse, if you can ever afford a holiday on nurses pay, go to the Costa Brava. Have you ever been abroad?" I mentioned that I had been to Switzerland once and he asked me all about it. What was the skiing like, the accommodation, the company. I got so enthusiastic in my replies that all my nerves disappeared, so when he said. "What do you know about Christmas disease?" I was taken aback. There was just enough time to describe the disease and it's treatment when the bell rang to end the examination. I have often wondered how he marked that one question, but I got a pass mark. I learned afterwards that he thought nurses should be concerned with nursing, not with the ins and outs of all the diseases in the book.

Patients often try to express their gratitude by giving nurses little presents. We do not accept gifts of money, but often a patient will leave a bar of chocolate or some fruit for the nursing staff. There were two patients on the women's ward, Mrs Lane, and Mrs Lamb. They were in opposite beds and were in for similar operations. One visiting time Mrs Lane's husband brought her a new bed jacket. It was beautifully made and we all admired it. Perhaps a bit too openly, for a few days later, Mrs Lamb's husband brought one in for her. It was another very pretty one, and obviously expensive. No one thought much about it after admiring it at first. Next, Mr Lane brought a bunch of red roses for his wife. Within two days, Mrs Lamb had a bigger bunch delivered. After one or two little incidents like this we began to realise there was a bit of rivalry between the two women. One day I was bathing Mrs Lamb, and she took a huge pear out of her locker. "Here nurse, this is for you." I thanked her and put it to one side to take when I went off duty. Ten minutes later, when I was bathing Mrs Lane, she took out a box of chocolates.

"Have these, nurse," she said. Thanking her also, I put them with the pear. Over the next few days the nursing staff gained tremendously from the rivalry between Mrs Lane and Mrs Lamb. They were both discharged on the same day, and within a week a parcel arrived at Sister's office containing a 2lb tin of toffees for the nurses from Mrs Lamb. She was obviously intending to have the last word. The day after that another parcel arrived, this contained an identical tin of toffees from Mrs Lane. We enjoyed them, and voted the competition a draw in the absence of the competitors.

One evening we were all in the flat, a fairly rare thing for us, when the doorbell rang. Evelyn answered and a few minutes later she ushered in two quite presentable young men. They were complete strangers to us and we wondered why she had invited them in. It turned out that they were insurance brokers. At great length they explained to us the mechanics of insurance, how we would gain by buying a policy and how we would be covered in the event of accident or sudden death. They left us with piles of leaflets explaining everything anyone could ask about and left, promising to return the following week to see what we had decided. Although we were not unduly bothered about insurance, we thought it would be as well to encourage them, after all, they looked quite eligible. They came the following week and stayed for about an hour. We covered every aspect of an endowment policy, and we were getting to the stage of awkward silences because there was no more to talk about. We said we still needed a bit more time to make up our minds so they promised to call the following week. They came back the third week and Evelyn, because she had a keener conscience than the rest of us, agreed to buy a policy. Ian, the first insurance man opened his brief case and produced three large white forms. He told her that some of the questions asked by the insurance firm were of a personal nature, and if she would prefer the interview to be held in private, we could go into another room. Evelyn said that we all knew each other's business, anyway, so it didn't matter. Then it came, a barrage of questions, one after another covering every possible aspect of Evelyn's health and future prospects. Somewhat breathless, she sat back when he had finished the questions. Then another bombshell. "Now, Miss Morton, perhaps a little deposit to seal the contract." For a moment there was a look of consternation on Evelyn's face, then she remembered the rent, hidden in the desk drawer. Thus Evelyn became insured. The rest of us managed to avoid their persuasions although they came regularly and expectantly for another four or five weeks. Eventually we took to going out when they were expected or ignoring the bell.

Miss Mountford was an old lady admitted to Monmouth ward via Casualty. She was a spinster and lived alone in a little cottage. She had fallen and fractured her femur. A passer by, hearing her calls for help went and found her on the hall floor. She was weak and frail due to years of malnourishment. Making do with a sandwich instead of a proper meal had worn down her resistance and she was extremely ill. I was on Monmouth Ward the night she had a stroke. It had been a quiet night. No admissions, no emergencies, and I was lulled into a sense of false security. Consequently, I was unprepared for the sight that met me as I walked down the Ward. Only the traction on the injured leg was keeping her in bed. She had fallen sideways, like a log. Unconscious and motionless, the right side of her face lax and sagging. All the other patients were asleep. It must have happened suddenly and quietly. I could see as I got her into bed that cerebral damage was extensive. I called the Houseman. We did what we could and made her comfortable, but we both knew that in spite of all we could do, there wasn't much of a chance. The bed was empty when I came on duty the next night.

This was the start of a busy run, as so often happens. My next six weeks were hectic. I don't think I had time for coffee the whole time. There were five children's cots adjoining Monmouth Ward, where we put children who were in for endocrine investigations and any obscure things that required lots of tests. One night we had a haemophiliac in. He was about eight years old, Simon was his name. He had fallen and bruised his knee, starting a haemorrhage into the joint. We had to keep him completely quiet because every time he moved too much the bleeding would start again. To keep an eight year old boy quiet is not an easy task, especially when there are four other seemingly healthy children on the ward. Those children were marvellous, though. They seemed to sense the importance of keeping Simon still and quiet. They would sit by his bed and talk to him, they would read to him from their picture books and draw pictures for him with their crayons. One of the parents brought in a slide projector which kept them amused for days. Eventually the bleeding stopped and gradually we got Simon up and about. He was discharged in a few weeks with warnings to his parents to keep an eye on him and keep him out of mischief. An impossible task, and one I didn't envy them.

Chapter 11

State finals were looming up, Hospital finals, a kind of preparation for state finals with a hospital badge as a reward, were over. The results of these we knew within a week. We all passed. Jubilation and parties all round, and a week of general relaxation and a letting off of steam before we settled down to concentrate again.

Medicine, Surgery, Practical nursing, Viva Vox, Psychiatric, Obstetric, Fevers, Gynaecology, Ear Nose and Throat, Radiology, Theatre technique, Plastic Surgery, Cardiac Surgery, … The list was endless. We had to know enough about all these subjects and about twenty others unlisted to be able to answer random questions on any one of them. We might only have questions on appendicitis and things in the surgical paper, but we had to have a working knowledge of all the other things, just in case. The real academics among us, as well as knowing all the routine things, found time to swot up on bacteriology and metabolism, too. There was one girl in our set, a little older than the rest of us, who had a BA degree. She had gone to university as a natural progression from school, had drifted into university, gained a BA, and drifted out again.

The sad thing was that, although she was kind and the patients liked her, as a practical nurse she was hopeless. She will probably end up as a Matron or a social worker where she can give full reign to her administrative abilities. I remember once asking her why she hadn't trained as a doctor. She replied that although she found it comparatively easy to gain a BA, she felt she was incapable of mastering the scientific side of medicine. Whether this was true or not, we all went to Christine with our exam problems. Book work came naturally to her. She could remember facts that the rest of us had never even registered. She would listen to a lecture or read a chapter once, and she knew it, but Oh! The bruises she left after giving injections and the bandages which just would not stay on.

After weeks of frantic swotting far into the night, interspersed with periods of utter despair when we realised just how much we were expected to know, finals arrived. One week there was plenty of time, the next week they were upon us. I enjoyed them!

The anticipation and trepidation leading up to exams is almost unbearable. The exams themselves are a relief. There is the psychological knowledge that things are moving at last. Instead of weeks and weeks of taking in and assimilating facts, at last the person is giving out. There is also awareness that, with every paper finished, a milestone is passed. The few days the exams last, the pace is so fast that there is no time for post mortems and recriminations. The six weeks of waiting for results is another trying time, a time for doubts. By the time the six weeks of waiting were over seven out of ten of us were convinced we had failed.

It is a tradition where I trained, that on the morning the results came out we all trooped down to the post office, with some proof of identity, to collect the letter before the normal postal delivery. This entailed getting up at some unearthly hour of the morning. A thin letter told you that you had passed, and a thick one told you that you had failed, because it contained the application forms to try again. I felt my letter. It was thick. If I had failed, I thought, I would creep off somewhere and open it on my own. Gradually I became aware of the silence and the stricken faces all around me. We all had thick letters. Could this be 100percent failure? "Well," said Jane Parry, forthright to the last. "Let's know the worst," and tore open her letter. There was a brief note of congratulation, a form to apply for an SRN's badge, a uniform permit, a bulky list of rules and regulations - what was and was not considered ethical, and the printed address of the Royal College of Nursing. For once Jane was speechless, but her face told us the good news. We all opened our letters then. Thirty passes and unfortunately three failures. Whoever had spread the rumour that a thick letter meant failure! I sailed home on a cloud - honestly, it wasn't a green corporation bus - to be met by my very new husband. "We're going to Cyprus in six weeks," he said. That was twenty years ago. I've spent less than

4 years in England since then, Cyprus, Berlin, Malta. One day I might settle down and nurse.

Epilogue

Since that last sentence, another 30 years have passed. Add to the closing sentence Singapore, Hannover, Herford, and currently France, working as a nurse in most of these places until retirement in 1998. Since those far off days when I embarked on this project, a lot has changed. For example, vaccination against nearly all the childhood diseases, the worldwide elimination of smallpox, computerised patient procedures, keyhole surgery. The human genome has been discovered, forging highways into genetic research. Vast strides into infertility, and even human cloning is being discussed. The advent of decimalisation, the euro, metric measurements instead of imperial, mobile phones, tablet computers. All of these were almost unheard of when I trained. We do live in exciting times.

Also available by the author on Amazon

The Quota. A young adult thriller about a damaged young man who collects dolls - human dolls. His quota is four. Read what happens when he has collected all four of them...

B009QL4II

Sarah Sunshine and the Elves. A children's bedtime book with easy short chapters. Sarah Sunshine knew there were elves, she just didn't know where to find them. Follow her in her quest to locate their den and read about her adventures on the way.

B00881DJRM

Printed in Great Britain
by Amazon